CECIL BEATON'S FAIR LADY

ALSO BY CECIL BEATON

The Glass of Fashion
It Gives Me Great Pleasure
The Face of the World
Japanese
The Wandering Years
My Royal Past
Quail in Aspic
Images
Royal Portraits

Cecil Beaton's

FAIR LADY

HENRY HOLT AND COMPANY
NEW YORK

TO JACK WARNER WITH
GRATITUDE

INTRODUCTION

To work on a project such as *My Fair Lady* is to have the greatest creative experience that anyone working in the theatre can enjoy. To feel, from its inception, that all the elements are right, to know that each collaborator is as brilliant as another, and that one is on one's mettle to do only to the best of one's ability, is something very rare; in fact, it is that marvellous – but elusive – goal at which we are always aiming. It is very seldom that the mark is dead centre on the bull's-eye, but when the miracle happens it more than compensates for all the wide misses, those doomed 'try-outs' in the provinces, the bleak, all-night rehearsals in cold Manchester theatres, and even the journeys to Newhaven in cattle trucks to be followed by bad notices and short runs.

At the time that Herman Levin approached me about doing the costumes for a musical version of *Pygmalion* I was still bathing my wounds from the ordeal of having been involved in designing sets and costumes for a play that proved to be one of those unhappy experiences in the theatre. Even if one's hopes are hoisted high, one can never take for granted that the path of production will run smooth. I remember once writing enthusiastically to Lynn Fontanne about the prospect of working with her on a new play, Coward's *Quadrille*. 'It will be such fun,' I wrote. She wryly replied, 'It will be a lot of hard work – anxiety – worry. We will very likely fight to the death, we hope to win through to success, but it won't be fun.' In fact, one can generalize that the production in which all is harmonious, when never a voice is raised in anger and all is finished on schedule, is the play that closes on Saturday night, or, in movies, is the motion picture that is never heard of again. My participation in this particular comedy was one of those misbegotten ventures that one makes through a mistaken notion of helping a friend. The result was not only the loss of that friend and – worse – a whole summer, but the birth of a conviction that no theatre success should be gained at the cost of so much acrimony, chicanery, and ruthless cruelty as had gone into bludgeoning this charming, but rather fragile little comedy into a Broadway near-hit.

If Herman had not brought Lerner and Loewe into my life at this psychological moment I firmly believe, so great was my fear of finding myself again bound by contract, that I would have given up designing for the theatre. But when Fritz Loewe, at Claridges, played and sang to me the first songs he had composed for his musical *Pygmalion* I was immediately under the spell of his extraordinary talent. By this time he was, with hair flying, eyes popping, and whole frame jerking in a state of euphoria, thumping out the rumba rhythm and singing Alan Lerner's lyrics for 'The Rain in Spain', I knew nothing in the world would prevent me from working on this show.

A few years back, soon after the war, the Theater Guild of America, in the form of the late Lawrence Langner and his wife, Armina Marshall, had come to my crimson-curtained study in London to discuss my doing the designs for a musical to be made from the same Shaw play. They considered that Eliza would create a wonderful song-and-dance role for Gertrude Lawrence. We huddled over the fire, but somehow the necessary spark of enthusiasm was not kindled in my imagination: I could not visualize the metamorphosis of this play into terms of operetta. The production never materialized. Now, in a flash, I could see how Lerner and Loewe's transformation from straight to musical play should look. The more I thought about it, the more I was enthusiastic about the wish-fulfilling opportunity to re-create the world as I remembered it when *Pygmalion* first appeared in 1914.

I had, in fact, never seen the play in its first stage production, but I well remember, as a schoolboy, the excitement at the Haymarket, at the end of the second act, caused by Mrs Patrick Campbell's using a blasphemous word never heard on the English stage. When the play was published in a monthly magazine, I was recuperating, among the adult splendours of a seaside hotel in England, from an attack of scarlet fever.

One of the hotel guests was an extremely glamorous American girl. I watched with eagerness her every appearance, the variety of her clothes, the panniers on her taffeta skirts, her Dolly Varden hats and Elizabethan collars. I was aglow with admiration at the way her dun-coloured hair was curled high in what, today, we call a beehive. It was through *Pygmalion* that I got to know this lady.

'Would you care to read this play?' I asked her. 'It has caused a sensation because the leading lady uses the word "bloody".' The American girl was astonished by the superficial sophistication of this ten-year-old.

Now, forty-two years later, I saw an opportunity to re-create the excitement inspired by the American girl in the hotel and, indeed, all the fashions of the period that had so impressed me in boyhood.

At first the Producer, Herman Levin, and the Director, Moss Hart, had considered that our venture should be costumed in the period around 1904. This was the epoch in which all recent musicals had automatically been costumed, no doubt because of the similarity with the present fashion in up-swept hairstyles and tight-fitting bodices which, it was considered, would ingratiate audiences, and portray that 'never never land' with less of a jolt than some less familiar look. But so frantic was my appeal for the re-creation of the world I knew before it disappeared in the first World War, that I was given the reins. 'Just so long as you're sure the girls will look attractive and sexy,' said my friend Herman. When I told Moss of my intention to make Ascot entirely black and white – an idea that had originated with the famous Black Ascot after King Edward's death – he was worried. 'You're sure it won't look like a comic strip?' But, luckily, further fears were kept from me, so that I went to work with the greatest fervour. Never had any theatre assignment given me so much pleasure. Suddenly, a myriad childhood's impressions were paying dividends: haphazard pieces of the jig-saw puzzle of memory suddenly started sorting themselves into place. Remembered, for example, was that, when I was about five years old, Miss Elfie Perry, 'the first actress I had ever met', had come to dinner wearing a frock of striped silk. Of course that would be perfect for Eliza's last appearance. Madame Triana, an enormous elephant of a woman, had eaten an ice-cream in a marquee at a garden party given by my Aunt Jessie, wearing a dress of grey and apricot: this colour combination I would certainly use. Mrs Higgins must wear the Malmaison, with circular pink cardboard back-reinforcement, that my mother wore with her grey satin and ostrich feathers at Ascot. Shades of my mother, my Aunt Jessie, shades of my first theatre goddess – Lily Elsie, Gaby Deslys and Mrs Vernon Castle!

Not only I but everyone else connected with the production, became more elated as each new element was brought into line. Rex Harrison, nervous about appearing in a musical for the first time, at last signed to appear. The casting of Stanley Holloway as Doolittle was nothing short of masterly. New York audiences had been conquered by Julie Andrews' delicious comedic qualities in *The Boy Friend*, and she seemed to be a godsend for the part of the very young Eliza. When, on the initial day of rehearsal under Moss' friendly guidance, the cast and all contributors were introduced to one another, the feeling was unique: each song was received by the cast with spontaneous applause – applause which became more thunderous as the morning progressed. Everyone was fired with excitement. Rehearsals immediately started with the most remarkable and unquestioned conviction that this was to be a show to beat all shows.

This enthusiasm continued and carried us through snowstorms, blizzards and endless nights of dress-rehearsals at Newhaven. Temperament outbursts were confined to only one member of the cast, and the usual bitter pains of re-writing and cutting scenes (one whole ballet and one of Eliza's most enchanting songs were eliminated) were stoically endured. For everyone was fortified with the knowledge that grew each week that here was a unique production that created theatre magic.

When the musical opened in New York, a new page was turned in the annals of the stage. The performance of the first night audience was almost as great as that on the stage. Every nuance appreciated, the perfect crack of applause rewarded every big effect. The subsequent rush for seats is part of theatrical history. For eight years the musical play has continued in different countries of the world. Eliza, dressed like Elfie Perry, appeared in England, Argentine, Australia, New Zealand, South Africa, Mexico, Russia, Holland, Norway, Denmark, Finland, Iceland, Italy, Sweden, Israel and Japan. Rumours about the making of a film persisted. Then, in an explosive moment of excitement, all was arranged. Warner's had bought the property for a record price of five million dollars and shooting would start in 1963. Alan Lerner was to supervise and write the screenplay, and of the original cast Rex Harrison and Stanley Holloway were signed. Audrey Hepburn was to be the screen Eliza. I was to be in charge of the costumes, sets and the whole of the visual production.

Most people have strangely vague ideas about a designer's job in films or the theatre. They consider, perhaps, that a certain person is brought in to supply his favourite colour schemes, to exert his personal preferences indiscriminately in fabric and furnishings. In fact, the designer's domain is far-reaching. His job is to paint the story, to supply in shapes, light and colour, the plastic aspects of the play. The harmonies and dissonances of shape and colour are as important to a film, particularly a musical film, as is the orchestration of the instruments to the composer of a symphony.

He must produce the taste of each character and each scene itself in terms of clothing and surroundings. He must give emphasis to all words and changes, perhaps even perform the miracle of showing the different states of mind of specific characters even when not changing their clothes. He has reality at his command to suit to the occasion – to be lessened or heightened as the pitch or requirements of the story dictate.

Because the designs of sets and costumes can only affect the visual mood to a limited extent, the amount that he is able to do is therefore all the more determined by his own tenacity, ability, imagination and experience. Because of its very limitation, the designer's work requires more style and experience than that of a more important ingredient.

When the high notes are sung every object that meets the eye shall soar, if possible, with the sounds that reach the ear. Ideally everything – words, voices, movements, hands, feet, dresses, hats, trousers, doorways, roof-tops, ceilings and chandeliers – should unite in every detail to create that sudden blaze, that exultant climax of perfection which draws the audience into its triumphant updraught.

With such rich materials as *My Fair Lady* offered, the difficulties of designing became an incentive and a delight; they promised one of the richest experiences of my stage career.

ILLUSTRATIONS

LONDON

George Cukor tornadoed into my London house. Cukor, of Hungarian origin (his name means 'sugar'), with brown eyes flashing through spectacles, a wide mouth frequently displaying seven lower incisors, had already directed forty Hollywood moving pictures. Like most Hollywood arrivals, his was an eleventh hour one. It had been five o'clock in the morning when I got back from Venice to meet him but George, fortunately, did not seem to notice my somewhat 'piano' mood nor, in fact, to take in his surroundings, so full was he of his love of animals, his own dogs in Hollywood in particular, and of how people who loved dogs were generally nice, while women who did not like dogs were fundamentally bitches. He was obviously over-excited at our first meeting on this great project: he was to be Director of the film version – so eagerly awaited – of *My Fair Lady*. He talked non-stop. He did not talk exclusively on our mutual project, but on a variety of diversified subjects. My pencil was poised to write down the answers to a few specific questions: 'When do we start work?' 'Where do we work?' 'Do I do my research here in England?' 'When do we start shooting, and how long is the schedule?' 'You *do* want the period to be pre-war, 1914, and I suppose Ascot *is* to be black and white?' But my notebook remained blank as George told me about the Ethel Barrymore Foundation and Marilyn Monroe's suicide. On his way back to the Savoy Hotel we drove to Baron's Court to cast an eye at some studios which were built soon after the turn of the century. They may give us a clue to our 'street where Higgins lives' as they strike me as being somewhat in Fabian taste. I enthused: 'The RIBA has a marvellous book on houses for "artistic people with small incomes" by Baillie Scott; we ought to use some of Voysey's designs for Mrs Higgins' house.' 'Yes, yes, we have great research in Hollywood.' 'But,' I replied, 'I doubt if you'd see interiors like these anywhere else. And we must also go and see Norman Shaw's houses at Bedford Park – they are typically and uniquely English.' 'Yes, yes, we'll get them all photographed – inside and out. I generally do that when I'm working on a picture. You remember when I was doing *Les Girls*, you arranged for us to photograph every detail of Loelia Westminster's apartment? We photographed every God-damned thing in that flat.' 'Yes, she was very surprised to come home one afternoon to find two men photographing her fire-irons.' 'At any rate we used some interesting bits: her tapestry needlework frame and the drink tray and two telephones. Ah yes, yes, these houses – yes! They're called St Paul's Studios, and this is Baron's Court. Let me make a note of that. I always make a note of everything, and my pockets are full of bits of paper. Can you give me a bit of paper? Now, how do you spell Talgarth? T-A-L-G-A-R-T-H Road? Well, we'll meet up tomorrow with Gene Allen,★ and you show him these. Yes, very interesting. And, by the way, what is the name of your florist, and would they send a plant to Vivien Leigh at Uckfield, Tickerage Mill, Blackboys – isn't that a wonderful name! – and you wouldn't like to come to Constantinople with me, would you? Well, do you know anyone in Constantinople? No, well, never mind! Perhaps we can meet on my way back in Paris. Now, when will I be in Paris? I've it written down somewhere. I'll call you and tell you when I'm going to be at the hotel . . . what is it called? Plaza Athénée, yes, that's it! I'll be at the Plaza Athénée on . . . well, I'll call you in the morning. We can go and see Audrey in Paris – she's crazy to play the part, you know. She says she has always been dying for you to do her costumes, but she has just one suggestion to make about Eliza's first appearance – she doesn't want to dictate, but wondered whether, instead of your just fitting her into something so well known, you couldn't give her a little characterization? But only if you think it suitable. She's an adorable kid, and she's not being difficult. Perhaps we can come back to London from there together? I *am* coming back to London

★ He was to help me with sets as Assistant Designer, and he had arrived with George Cukor.

to see – oh! I can't remember his name – yes, an actor – I've it written down somewhere. By the way, what stomach medicine do you recommend if I should get the old trots in Constantinople? Oh, I'll have to write that down – no, you can tell it to me tomorrow. We'll meet at what time? Well, we'll arrange everything in the morning.'

Tuesday, 11 September

The market was almost deserted this evening except for a few policemen hanging around in the empty, reverberating arcades. George, Gene Allen and I were wandering round Covent Garden, looking for locations and 'local colour', before having a squint at the evening performance of *My Fair Lady* at near-by Drury Lane. I wanted Cukor to be impressed by everything he saw in order to overcome his dislike of making pictures in England, ("They're always breaking for cups of tea.'). I felt so positively that many scenes, particularly the cockney ones, must be photographed within the sound of Bow Bells. George said: 'Yes, yes, we will certainly shoot some of the scenes here,' but he seemed to be in need of extra conviction. I tried my hardest to stage-manage the outing, but the lack of market life at this hour struck me as a personal affront. Moreover, as often happens when one assumes a responsibility for everything that one is showing off, I even had trouble in locating certain favourite landmarks: 'I *think* St Paul's church is at the end of this arcade, but just in case it isn't, I'll ask this policeman.' 'You're a fine guide,' said George. But he was impressed by the scale of the columns of St Paul's while I noticed, with certain misgivings, that they had recently been so cleaned that they no longer looked as if they were made of the droppings of a million pigeons. Gene Allen, a former policeman, stocky, apple-faced, with a bullet head and child's starry eyes of wonderment, agreed that an effective shot could be taken of the Opera House façade, with the green wrought-iron framework of the market buildings alongside. My fears that the real London might not be used were momentarily allayed. By degrees, the semblance of a beginning for the film formulated itself.

Watching *My Fair Lady* tonight was for me like witnessing the laying-out of a friend. After playing for five years all life had gone from the performance; there remained a tired old show with seemingly too few musicians in the orchestra pit and not enough people in the chorus to furnish the stage. Even the lights seemed to lack their former lustre. Zena Dare, who at the age of seventy has clocked in at almost every performance for the entire run, was having a fortnight's holiday. Many of the cast were understudies of understudies, and while waiting for their big opportunity, appeared to have grown disastrously old. Eliza had wilted, and when she was arriving at Ascot it seemed as if her feet hurt. Mrs Pearce, the housekeeper, was the only character who gave any reality to what she was saying. It was particularly painful for me to see that the clothes, over which so much trouble had

originally been taken, and which were chosen according to each actor's personality, had not only been sent to the cleaners until their goodness had long since departed (some of the materials were as shiny as lacquer), but were being worn by a cast that had changed so often that no resemblance remained to the originals. The capacity audience fortunately did not share my disappointment. They responded just as they were meant to, but the laughs came, not from the wit of Shaw's lines, but from some awful 'business' that had been interpolated in the absence of a director: Doolittle tripping up on his first entrance, squashing a bug with his foot, Higgins catching a flea and indulging in tasteless horse-play when showing embarrassment.

The life of a play in any one production is always limited. Comes a moment when the bloom is off. This particular production was long since dead except, of course, at the box office. The funeral parlour activities on stage produced in me such chronic physical discomfort that I begged permission to leave after Eliza's success at the ball.

Thursday, 13 September

This was the peak moment of activity: barrows wheeling intricately, lorries backing dexterously; a climate of hurry and opulence; flowers effulgent, fruit succulent, and shining vegetables immaculately packed and unpacked by loving, reverent hands; boxes of plants whizzing through the air to be caught deftly and displayed in racks on high; much jovial skylarking; a cigarette accepted and placed behind an ear for later; all noises echoing thunderously under the hollow dome. 'Wouldn't those mounds of carrots be rather a good background for a small scene?' I asked. 'Yes,' George Cukor replied, 'we have vegetables like that down-town in the Farmers' Market.' 'Get that old woman's hat!' he pointed: 'That's the sort of feel we want in the cockney clothes.' 'Yes – Bermans of Leicester Square can rout out all sorts of tatty little tippets, fur coatees and Victoriana from the real sources,' I suggested. 'Oh, but you should see Western Costumes! They have everything!'

The variety of accents around us made Professor Higginses of us all, and we were fascinated by the voices at the coffee and breakfast stalls. However, the greatest surprise to Cukor and Allen was the fact that no one appeared badly dressed or down-at-heel. The men running the stalls were like bank managers, and even the barrow pushers were Teddy Boys, elegantly dressed.

This over-all impression that the Dickensian squalor of dark alleyways, the refuse-lined, subterranean passages of Stepney, have long since disappeared from London was further emphasized this afternoon, Driving, somewhat ridiculously, in a vast Queen Mary limousine rented by Warner Brothers, George, Gene and I gingerly explored the East End.

'But where are the real slums?' George asked. 'No one's dirty! These rows of houses are all neatly painted! The apartment-houses are much too luxurious with their window-boxes, balconies, telly aerials and pastel colours! All the children are dressed like Princess Anne!'

I was amused at the idea of trying to show the worst instead of the best, of my doing an inverse Potemkin tour with Cukor as Catherine of Russia. Instead of showing off cardboard villages with idyllic villagers dancing on the green, I was endeavouring to demonstrate the squalors of Limehouse, Bermondsey and Bethnal Green. 'There's been a social revolution!' shouted George in disgust. 'This is the never-had-it-so-good epoch all right. Ah, there's a bit! Under that railway arch – that's nearer the thing we want.' Frowning faces peered, by no means reassured that the hoped-for degree of squalor had been vouchsafed them. 'Ah, now, this is better! That's rather a messy street; is that a dead cat? Oh, no! – But look how well dressed that woman is: she's off to do her shopping. Well, we'll have to go to the Mexican quarter in Los Angeles; there we will find the real thing!'

Friday, 14 September

George Cukor and Gene Allen were waiting at the main entrance of the Savoy Hotel when I arrived six minutes late for an expedition to hunt for locations. We were to be accompanied by a research photographer, but the photographer was missing. Where the hell was he?

Meanwhile, George sorted pieces of paper from his pockets. 'Dr Collis' Stomach Drops, what is this? Oh yes, yes! Talgarth Road? Yes, yes. Yes. Now the contrast today between great and small, rich and poor, is so little, but was then so great. You know, Higgins really achieved a miracle in passing Eliza off. We've got to make that point clearly – of the two worlds apart – and the contrast of class distinction in an age now seemingly pre-historic. But where in Christ is the research photographer?'

Without him we started off to prospect in Wimpole Street ('On The Street Where You Live') where my own physician, Dr Gottfried, lives, at number 75. Many of these houses, with their decorative windows of frosted glass and individual doorways of no accepted style, could certainly have belonged to Professor Higgins. But how could we stem the tide of patients arriving every minute to see some specialist, and rope off such a busy, important street even for one day? That's for the Company to arrange. Meanwhile, Cukor asked, couldn't we ring any front-door bell and ask if we might come and have a look at their fire-irons?

With the recent rash of robberies total strangers were not likely to be well received, and the three of us did not present a particularly confidence-inspiring spectacle.

I decided that Dr Gottfried, who, in the days before he left Vienna, had dealings with theatre and opera artists, would be sympathetic to this sudden intrusion. He was amused and intrigued as he showed us around, as, indeed, were all the other occupants of the house, who, by degrees, heard the still-magic word 'Hollywood', and appeared at every door on every floor. Some were dismayed at the attention given to an impromptu cupboard, a gimcrack partition or inglenook. So entirely suitable for our purpose did this house appear that we decided to copy it in almost all essentials. Permission was granted to photograph and measure every detail from the servants' basement to attic bedrooms.

After many telephone calls, and an hour of valuable early morning time was wasted, the misunderstanding of the missing research photographer was explained: he had been waiting at the Embankment entrance of the Savoy Hotel. I was grieved to hear Cukor say: 'It's things like this that make me foam at the mouth at the very idea of making a picture in England!' Of course, it's only natural that George should feel more at ease working on his home ground, and using studios that he knows well. But Italian and Russian films have accustomed us to such authenticity of atmosphere that even in musicals the 'local colour' must be real. I wondered if this essentially 'London' musical could be done entirely on the back lot at Warner's? George was reassuring. 'Of course we will do *some* of it here. Now show Gene those studios we went to the other night.' From Baron's Court I acted as cicerone to Bedford Park, Chiswick and Turnham Green. We gawked at Voysey houses, the Tabard Inn with its William de Morgan tiles, and St Michael's hideous William Morris-y Church.

Gene Allen returned to Hollywood, and George Cukor, with Dr Collis' Stomach Drops, left for the Orient. Meanwhile, the London office of Warner's would send out scouts in every direction, trying to find Hogarthian slums. June Osborn and some of her dedicated 'good deed' workers in the East End, together with

John Betjeman, made a tour of Islington for real squalor, but the report came back that not a bushel of dirt was to be found. Unexpectedly, Dr Gottfried had come across some rather picturesque poverty when driving through Kilburn.

George sent me an amended itinerary: 'Will be in Paris 24th, not the 23rd, arriving London 29th.' Ten days later I heard from a mutual friend that Cukor would not be returning to London. Warner's wanted him in Hollywood, but when I spoke to him on the telephone he reiterated that he would be back – he would be back!!

Friday, 15 February 1963

It seemed strange to find myself packing possibly for a whole year in California while London remains blanketed with snow and ice. The entire day was feverish. Earlier, with traffic around Covent Garden almost at a standstill, I had been caught in a taxi. Got out and ran to the Opera House where I was finishing work on two productions simultaneously, an opera and a ballet. Across the road in the Wardrobe, Nureyev had arrived for his final fittings. We anticipated difficulties because Nureyev had not ingratiated himself with the staff and had crossed swords with a harassed tailor. In the morning I had to be in the scene-painting shop for vital, last-minute decisions about *Turandot*; unexpectedly, Margot Fonteyn had burst in, wearing fur-topped boots, to suggest, with an innocent expression, that her country scene dress should be made of a different material. I had left to the last minute a visit to the City to see about my will; the proofs of the illustrations of my latest book had to be checked with Mark Boxer; the BBC interviewed on tape Freddie Ashton and me; I had my hair cut, and Princess Margaret came to lunch.

HOLLYWOOD

The police cop at the auto gate at Warner Brothers' Studio laughed and waved wildly at George Cukor who drove me, in his shining black Rolls Royce, to the éclair-coloured bungalow on the lot which I was to share with him. But this was to be for me, also, a day of warm receptions. Gene Allen, the Art Director, materialized almost immediately with his bright, twinkling eyes, sparkling teeth and well-scrubbed cheeks. He seemed like an old friend after our days looking unsuccessfully for locations in London some months back.

Then George Hopkins, the Set Decorator, appeared. Lanky and Grant Wood-looking, he has a deep voice like gravel and the quick eyes of a cockatoo. His domain comprises the vast warehouses full of furniture of every period, the carpenter's shop where more furniture is made, and 'Upholstery' where, at his word, thousands of yards of material are made into curtains, bed, chair or sofa covers. Would I like my rooms done up? They once belonged to Harry Warner, but they are kind of gloomy now. 'Great!' 'What colour?' 'White.' 'Will do. And new curtains?' 'Orange, please.' 'Will bring patterns. And what colour carpet?' 'Grey.' When, by noontime, two painters in white overalls had already started work on the walls, I realized with what irrevocable speed things can be done in a studio.

Introduction to Joe Hiatt, in charge of 'Wardrobe', a dark, florid-faced giant with the eyes of a Renoir child. Little wonder that in such a vast factory as he showed me, they are anxious to make all the clothes for our picture. A programme had just been completed, and it was sad to see these efficiently-equipped rooms

19

for cobblers, tailors, dressmakers and dyers all deserted as if there had been a plague. Joe would now set about putting the whole works in motion again.

'Research' was like a University library. I wondered why, with all this brilliant documentation and with solicitous scholars at hand, most moving-pictures ignore authenticity. Mr Carl Millikin and his Viennese assistant, Gusti Adler, proceeded to send me every book they had on the pre-1914 war period decoration and fashion. Meanwhile, what could they order for me?

By now, the moment had arrived when I could be introduced to the hierarchy in the executive building. Steve Trilling, rosy-faced and enthusiastic, virtually runs the studio while Jack Warner is away, but Warner would be returning any day now. Meanwhile, great *bonhomie* and wisecracking: everyone smiling and happy. Such a welcome, and quite a change from England where an all-pervasive solemnity is likely to prevail. However, we will see if the hilarity is just part of a façade.

It was difficult to realize that any work was being done as George, Gene and I, lolling around, feet up, talked in a desultory manner. But, in fact, we were going through the script, scene by scene, deciding how to do the ballroom scene, or how to differentiate the houses of Mrs Higgins and her son. 'How would you react to my doing the ballroom in trellis? It was very fashionable in 1912 and would be a welcome relief from the usual gold and cream "Grace Kelly" sets.' Books arrived forthwith from Research, showing Elsie de Wolfe salons and lobbies done in 1910 in the fashionable lattice work. Gene, enthusiastic, produced a ravishing *treillage* room from Schönbrunn.

Wednesday, 20 February

To me it is still quite a shock to watch a movie at ten in the morning; somehow it gives a feeling of guilt to sit in the dark, oblivious of the sun outside. I feel the best part of the day is being squandered; this is so even when I tell myself that this is 'work'. It was also a surprise to hear George and Gene shouting a running commentary. This sparse and extremely critical audience, with no one to 'Shush' us, was judging the picture from purely technical standards: 'They might have gotten rid of her earlier.' 'Someone's done a poor job on that backing.' 'How many times have we seen *that* before?' 'Oh no, not that old candle gag again!'

Faults that were not apparent to me were seen by George's professional eye which is as quick as a safari spotter's. Neither did one detail of banal dialogue or unreal acting escape him. It was as if he has developed another sense.

We were watching the old *Pygmalion*, which I'd loved when I saw it twenty years ago. Wendy Hiller's truth and honesty still shine through the years. George was of the opinion that Leslie Howard's performance was too vindictive, alarming and even cruel; Rex Harrison would give the role a sweep of grandeur and the impression of being extraordinarily aristocratic in his attitude to everyone. To me the overwhelming impression of seeing this picture again was to realize the brilliance with which Lerner and Loewe had adapted their musical version.

Gene had also suggested we see *East of Eden* for the purpose of watching an attempt to overcome the limitations of the still crude and primitive era of colour photography in which we work. By confining the colours almost to monochrome, the effects were beautiful. We were heartened, for we knew that, at any rate, we also could achieve a negative effect that would be pleasing.

Jack Warner's eyes popped with apparent incredulity when he first caught sight of me, but he appeared relieved when I turned out to be more or less human after all, and laughed at his jokes: 'Hah, I've got a new audience.'

His shining teeth stretched wide, his eyebrows high in youthful surprise, his complexion clear and tanned, his hair shining, nut-brown, he caressed the length of his silk tie with well-manicured fingers. He is an amazingly agile figure, and holds himself with such a straight spine that sometimes he appears almost to be toppling backwards. In his yachting jacket and sportive shoes, he has something about his swashbuckling style that reminds me of Douglas Fairbanks, Senior, and the great era of silent movies. In fact, he is the sole remaining partner of Warner Brothers and, in spite of the aura of the vaudeville theatre in which his career started, the jocular gags with twirling cigars and schoolboy jokes, one sees that for every good reason he is still the head of one of the few great film empires to survive.

'Now, first we've got to tie Alan Lerner down. He's a difficult boy to get hold of, and we have to know when we can expect a finished script. If we don't start soon, time will envelop us. How's that for an ad-lib? I like that bit. Time will envelop us.'

At lunch in the executive room Warner gesticulated in the grand manner. 'This used to be Marion Davies' bungalow when W.R.* kept putting her in films, and we made them for him. He was like a Louis, that W.R. Did you ever sleep in Cardinal Richelieu's bed up at the ranch? Yes, he was a Louis all right.'

The dining-room is still decorated in the style of the twenties, with grisaille murals and pine panelling. The long table was set for about two dozen, with good silver, and an excellent meal was served. The 'top boys' were busy wisecracking and setting a good example by wearing suits, collars and ties. 'This is your brief moment of splendour, Ceesul,' George Cukor laughed: 'You'll never be asked in here again!'

Sitting next to Warner I made desperate attempts to talk on subjects that might interest him. I took pot-shots at Dali, polo, the Aga Khan and the old Embassy Club days in London. Warner's eyes were flashing towards the far end of the table, and his smile encompassed everyone, but I managed to keep him talking about James Dean. Jack Warner is foremost a tough businessman ('I may forget names but never a sum of money') but he showed that, in spite of all the chaff and nonsense, he recognized greatness. 'That kid Dean was a natural actor. He gave us a lot of trouble, but it was worth it! He only made three pictures, yet he had the biggest appeal of anyone at the box office. He was surrounded with stars in *Giant* but we believe he was twenty-five per cent responsible for the success of that picture! But boy, was he difficult! He slept in his dressing-room here, wouldn't quit. And he'd have broads in at all times of the night, and the police objected and said we were not insured against having people live in this "place of business", so we told Dean to quit. But he wouldn't. He was rather tight with his money. Then I said I'd pay his hotel, and still he wouldn't go, so we had to force him out physically. Then suddenly he started to become hysterical: he said he must return for a few minutes. Well, the police had to accompany him. When he was back in his room he put his hand in a pot and pulled out a thousand-dollar bill, and then another, and then another. He'd forgotten his money there.'

*W. R. Hearst.

The morning went by with diversions and interruptions. The only positive work, which lasted half an hour, consisted of making preliminary ground-plans for Higgins' house. Gene is practical and encouraging. We have used the three floors of Dr Gottfried's house in Wimpole Street which, with adaptations, suit Shaw's elaborate comings and goings. We chortled because we had really started. George Cukor cracked that he expected to see the job finished by the evening.

My afternoon was spent with pre-1914 war 'Studio Year Books', 'Gazette du Bon Ton' and Doré's 'London'. Doré's use of chiaroscuro is something we should try to use. Those brilliant contrasts of black on white and vice versa, all seen in a miasmic haze, are the quintessence of romanticism.

I am a parasite in George Cukor's room until the furnishings for my office arrive. We work in close harmony, and every aspect of the picture is discussed, from the style of lighting to be suggested in different scenes to the types of people who would be invited to the ball. George is in tearing spirits, and our bungalow rings with his laughter. Sometimes I am impatient and nervous to get some of my ideas on paper. But George is content to talk.

George likes to talk his ideas. He needs an audience. That's the way he works. He says he can't imagine my enjoying being by myself for hours upon end, closeted only with my drawings. With people around him, his ideas come twirling out of his brain like caramel on a revolving machine. His fingers twirl in the opposite direction to his eyes. Sometimes his mind rambles off in unexpected directions. Occasionally it is difficult to put together the missing links of the conversational chain.

Not only do I spend my entire day in George's rooms, together sharing a cold lunch off a card table, but he drives me to and from the studio, and is often generous enough to invite me to dine in his house. Not since the war have I seen so much of one person at a time. So far we get along well, but necessarily this must be a strain of endurance on both our parts. Can this possibly end in anything but tension?

It is sometimes hard to match George's enthusiasm, or to feel as violently on certain topics as he, especially as, by now, I know his repertoire almost verbatim. But if I am secretly judging him one moment I am, at the next, admiring him for his lack of inhibitions, his relish of things that make him laugh, and his essentially Christian virtues which include his leniency of attitude towards myself. I probably repeat myself as much as most, continually say things that rankle, must be quite a problem for him to be landed with. (After all, he did not choose me as his designer; I was possibly forced upon him as part of the deal.) Having someone who knew the whole play from the beginning, having experience of the discoveries and pitfalls in its inception, could be as irksome as it was helpful. But, so far, apart from admitting jealousy for the indestructible energy and tenacity of the British, George has shown no visible signs of disapproval or resentment.

Sudden action! Rhinehardt's Biedermeyer furniture, which had been re-upholstered for my own room, arrived from the prop department, along with easy-chairs, bulletin boards, Japanese cushions, etc. Empty sketchbooks – always a challenge – and impressive artists' materials of the latest inventions came in from the Art Department. I could now spread myself and get down to work.

What a relief, I not only have my rooms, but a secretary, pencils freshly sharpened every day, a carafe of iced water, a file for personal as well as business correspondence. I feel thoroughly spoiled, and now have someone to advise me and rely upon. In many ways, the first two weeks were a little baffling and, in spite of much kindness, reminded me of first term at boarding school.

Today was a first in using the telephone, learning which numbers to press for 'Hold', for 'Intercom', for outside or studio calls. I was rather slow, cut myself off while talking to Christopher Isherwood and called the Red Cross unit by mistake. But it was comforting to hear that my predecessor, Mr Harry Warner, had never, until the end of his days, learned which buttons to press.

It was altogether a day of 'firsts': a first, after a lifetime of using my father's cut-throat razor, to plug in and switch to an electric one: a first to take the wheel of the Chevrolet: a first to collect my weekly pay cheque, open a bank account and deposit the cheques.

Thursday, 28 February

Until I pass the California test, I am not legally permitted to drive a motor-car, so each morning a huge limousine arrives to bring

24

me to the studio. The drivers announce themselves by name. I go down to the hotel lobby to find Hal Rowan, a young buck in pale blue pants and cowboy boots. On the way to Burbank we talk about the industrial smog or the traffic rules. Next morning, the driver, Mike Lossiter, is a pock-marked, middle-aged man in shirt sleeves. We discuss the fantastic changes and growth that have taken place since we first came out to Hollywood in the 'thirties. We are passing a new group of impressive glass sky-scrapers. Even a few years ago this stretch of Sunset Boulevard was considered a waste lot, and land could be bought for practically nothing. This morning another driver announced: 'Mr Plumbrick: you'll know who I am – I'm wearing a bootonyeer.' He also wore a business suit and rimless glasses, and we talked about the policy of the studio, and Jack Warner's justifiable pride in being such a good citizen and influence in the industry.

It is all very pleasant and comfortable, but I long to show my independence and be able to drive where I will. I learnt quite a good deal from the official handbook about the rules of the road, but before I had really studied 'STOP!' I was summoned to take my driving test.

Mr Glover, of Warner's was most reassuring. He said that he would bring me again and again to the Department of Motor Vehicles in Hollywood until I fulfilled all their requirements. This is a great comfort for I have heard of grandmothers and children weeping and pleading hysterically on being told they have failed in their test and can never try it again. My finger-prints were taken and a flashlight went off for the photographic record only a few inches from my harassed face.

In the written test I failed when asked the significance of a solid double line in the centre of the road, and whether 25 mph is the correct speed for towing a trailer or passing a school bus.

When the police sergeant, sitting by my side in the car, instructed me to turn to the right, I turned, at the wrong moment, in the midst of a morass of traffic to the left. Mr Glover, from the curbstone, watched me with despair. This was only my first of many lesser mistakes. Gaining confidence, I wished to show the inspector that I had been motoring for a lifetime and drove casually at the rate of 35 mph in a residential district: this cost me more bad marks. But somehow I managed to win the day with 70 out of 100. Mr Glover's relief was as great as my own.

Two Assistant Directors, Buck Hall and Sergei Petschnikoff, have been assigned to the picture. Buck, wearing a scarlet sweater, looks like a vast ex-footballer in contrast to Petch, from darkest Hungary, who is elegant and urbane, with a kindly face of pumice stone and a crackling voice. Petch was asked to make a preliminary chart of the production, and for the first time we discussed the number of costumes to be made. One thousand!

I rang up Joe Hiatt, Head of Wardrobe, and asked if he would come and see me. I gave him a list of hard to find things which we would need. Then, going through the various documents from Research, I made rough notes of pertinent details: a window treatment, a high-backed chair, a tiered skirt. By degrees, a little progress.

Alan Lerner has materialized. George Cukor and I went to meet him in his Beverly Hills Hotel bungalow at 10 am. Alan, surrounded by managerial carnations, twisted cigarette stubs, coffee dregs, and a doctor at the 'ever ready' with vitamins, was elated at discovering he was not in the doghouse for his non-appearance. Soon we all went off in high spirits to the studio.

Alan is a real man-of-the-theatre. Without self-consciousness he sings and performs, moving around while his golden cigarette lighter falls to the ground, and inventing ninety new gags for laughs. After working in solitary confinement since his collaboration with Dick Rodgers came to an end, George, Gene Allen and I seem to trigger him off, and he enjoys our company. Always inventive and fertile of imagination, today he became inspired with all sorts of new scenes for the picture.

Steve Trilling came in. Alan had determined to be playfully aggressive as part of a defence mechanism. 'What have you done, Steve, about getting the musical director, André Previn?' Alan half-expected nothing had been done: in fact, Previn was on the line. I envied Alan his toughness, his directness and his blunt authority. I could do with a bit more of this.

Jack Warner then appeared and enthused about the transformation of my rooms. He kept up a running commentary which, for sheer vitality, was prodigious. He knew exactly what he wanted to say to all of us.

Warner, quite rightly, said he is not skimping us. Any reasonable request has been granted. 'But don't be unbusinesslike and spend needlessly through lack of organization. This is too important a picture for anyone not to do their best. It'll cost close to fifteen million. We're not behind schedule already, are we? No? Good!'

Warner stayed just long enough to give us the message that he was in charge and knew everything that was going on in his empire, including every detail of our plans. When he trotted out of the bungalow he was as fresh as a sixteen-year-old. But his vitality had been too much for us: he left us wrecks. George yawned. Alan collapsed. I had a headache.

Tuesday, 12 March

Work this morning was done at Alan's instigation around Cukor's pool while sunning ourselves. George does not care for this method of conferring and, today, looked more serious and eminent than I have ever known him. With wetted middle finger, he flicked through the script with rabid intensity. Today Alan was like a mosquito, but whenever swatted by George he managed to escape damage. Alan has a way of having his way. He wore a large silver halter around his neck, which reflects the sun into his face so that he becomes more sun-bronzed.

Many were the telephone calls he made, many were the cups of coffee he asked for, and many were the appointments he arranged before leaving for New York this afternoon. But Alan has perfect working manners. He never interrupts, has extraordinary patience and enthusiasm, is never tyrannical or rigid in his ideas, is always receptive to suggestions, and never the great author whose masterpiece cannot be improved.

Yet Alan has a sound reason for everything, and that includes any word he has written down. He seems to have a sixth sense about lyrics and knows the words of every song of the century. It is interesting to learn from him such things as: 'You must never hear a melody until it is sung.' 'Julie Andrews sang "Wouldn't It Be Loverly" as if she were telling a story with a different mood in every line.' 'The most important thing about a lyric is its rhythm.'

His pencilled notes, crossed out and amended, are like gold. In fact, they are, for he is a Midas in every sense; not only is he of an extremely wealthy family but, on his own initiative, has done quite well for himself.

Alan invented several little bits of business which will heighten the effect of a scene. Flailing the air with his enthusiastic arms, he said: 'It would be funny if Pickering's collar came undone.' 'It would be nice if the swinging-doors of the Winter Garden hit Rex on the ass.' 'We must see Audrey using her hands with the plants in a way we know she has learnt in the market.' 'And, in that last glimpse of her, before she leaves, reclining on a *chaise-longue*, she should look as if she could be eaten!'

George, imbibing the golden words, argued about one scene – the last between Mrs Higgins and Eliza: 'Doesn't it take away the suspense of wondering what has happened to Eliza if they are seen together?' Alan said: 'But the audience likes to be in the know. They'll laugh when Higgins suddenly sees Eliza and bellows "You!" '

Alan fled in a cloud of dust and small stones. The rest of us went to the studio, and life went on there with a little less exuberance.

Friday, 15 March

With Gene, I went through all the details of the various architectural elements to be incorporated in the Higgins' households: picking cornices, details of panellings, mouldings, balustrades and typical pieces of English *art nouveau* 1910.

It has taken us a month to collect our thoughts in trying to find a style to present Shaw as a film-musical, for this style must be consistent. We must romanticize the exteriors. The buildings will be imperceptibly elongated and painted in exaggerated light-contrasts to create a slightly-heightened effect to the ordinary.

Wimpole Street presents the greatest difficulties. When have you seen a studio street scene that is successful?

Things, at last, seemed to be moving when the 'illustrator', Ed Graves, sent in two gouaches of Covent Garden market as we are planning to reproduce it.

Looking through early bound copies of all the old magazines that were my Bible in the days when I first became stage-struck, I was re-living my youth. But today I saw my old favourites with jaundiced eyes. The photographs from the *Play Pictorial*, never good in themselves, now appeared utterly lifeless representations of lifeless plays without the illusion of the stage. So many dead relics. So many dead people. The back numbers of *Punch* were particularly ghost-haunted with the drawings of Lewis Baumer, Stampa and Haselden. Once I had considered the etiolated elegance of Shepperson's drawings the quintessence of poesie. But now they appeared surprisingly wooden. Yet the Belcher cartoons remain valid – so full of cockney guts and the gristle of poverty – and Bateman, apart from his cartoons, is still a devilishly good theatrical caricaturist.

Tuesday, 19 March

Men working on the road wear scarlet tunics so that they can be seen in the distance by onrushing motorists. In Italy or France the effect would be beautiful, but here the red has to be of that retina-irritant vermilion that has no guts, no body, no blood. The effect would not be so displeasing if the light of Southern California were less hard and brittle.

Here, the day-glow colours refuse to blend into the general *mêlée*, and assault the eyes with the individual onslaught of violence intended by the advertisers. The glitter of the Christmas reindeer and decorations strung across the top of Hollywood Boulevard, reflected in the burning sun of December, are a sickly reminder of what can happen when the colours of the spectrum are never muted by a blue haze – where twilight does not exist. It is not by colours, but by noting a date or hearing of some event, that one realizes the passage of the months. Nevertheless, somehow, today, there was a slight feeling of spring in the air. When I went to the sylvan suburbia of Bel-Air I noticed that a few trees were bursting into bud.

I had come to the Bel-Air Hotel to have a second look at an octagonal-ceilinged room. At first I had criticized the artificiality of these well-kept gardens with the captive swans and exotic, potted-out plants and shrubs. Perhaps already my taste has changed. On my arrival today all looked delectable. I decided it would give me a new lease of life to move here and make my home of a room looking on to this Disneyish courtyard with its clumps of banana trees, cushions of marguerites and papyrus fronds sprouting around the trickling Italian fountain. What matters it if at night the coloured lighting on the tropical Botanical

Gardens is made for Panorama, or if the chorus of frogs croaking, and the crickets, do come from a hidden sound track?

The time had now come for Cukor to see the rough drawings from which I will take my designs. After an enormous amount of research the sketches fill a fat book. With tremendous gusto George licked his centre finger, the better to turn and prod the pages. His eyes moved in rapid, almost invisible, jerky movements somewhat like an insect's.

When, at last, George thumbed through to the last page he screwed up his face. 'I didn't care for "The Rain In Spain" costume you did for Julie Andrews. We must make Audrey look slightly – er – er – comic in that scene, as if Mrs Pearce had been out and bought her a dress from – who's your Pear and Does? Jack Robinson? She should look clean but not *chic*, and that's going to be awfully difficult because Audrey looks *chic* in anything. Also, at Ascot she should seem somewhat – er – overpowered by her finery. She shouldn't be quite able to – er – carry it off. Try and devise a costume that will work dramatically to accentuate the comic content of the scene.'

George sometimes puts his head around the adjoining doors to our rooms and asks me peculiar requests on which I, being English, am supposed to be an authority. Today he asked me who would be at Ascot in 1913, and how would they behave? This is the sort of thing I would suggest:

'There would be lots of raucous gaiety and hearty laughter when two couples meet and make jolly jokes. Men flex their calves backwards and slap backs. Women roar with double chins and heads thrown back. Some women irritated with their veils tickling their nose or lips.

Among those present would be:

THE DUKE OF C. Like a bloated dropsical fish – red nose – stuttering with a cleft roof to his palate – wearing yellow carnation in buttonhole.

LORD R. Straight – with military manner and cold eyes peering with disdain at all women.

LORD L. A bedraggled but plucky cockatoo.

G., LADY N. A Boadicea skimming the waves with high, proud jaw, like a ship's figurehead.

COLONEL L. Hat over eyes – very racy and dashing, with gold watch chain.

COUNTESS OF G. Looking for a battle in a persevering way – like a shopper looking for bargains.

MRS O. L. T. Searching for slights – sycophantic smile – often meeting with the cut direct, then completely nonplussed.

LADY M. Gipsy-like – shortsighted, but busy with her race card – with her, betting is a serious business.'

Wednesday, 20 March

George called a meeting of 'Wardrobe', represented by Joe, Anne Laune, the Wardrobe production forelady, Eleanor Abbey, my

charming and talented assistant from London, and myself. Petch took notes. 'Now, about "extras", if you'll excuse the word,' said George, 'not a God-damned one in this world is going to have suntan makeup. They say it makes the eyes and teeth look white. Well, it looks damned awful, and everyone on the lot has it. They just look as if they'd fallen into a puddle of mud and not been dried off. When we have the cockneys in, we'll tell them we want them to look God-awful. If they don't like it they can get their asses out. I don't want anyone covered with lipstick saying: "I've got no makeup on." Kick their asses out. They must look naked, scrubbed, take everything off them! If they've got false teeth, take 'em out. And I want you to start looking right now for old clothes to wear in Covent Garden – old used clothes, not just things that are dirtied up by the prop man, but real old, worn materials, and masses of them: vests and shirts and jerseys and coats on coats, and lots of petticoats under skirts. We've been going through books and books and books, and the poor people wore so much, layer on layer, and shawls on top of everything.'

Petch had a problem. 'How, in July, are we going to keep them from perspiring in the heat? It'll show, you know.' He looked very sad. But George's head was buried in a book, *London at the Turn of the Century*. 'Well, that's your problem. I can't guarantee to have those God-damned people cool.'

Since organization was in the air, and the moment seemed a sympathetic one, I told George of my serious misgivings about not being left in peace to get on with my designs. If the present pressure continued and heads popped around my door at all times of the day, I would be behind schedule. It takes real concentration to get down on paper all there is to do before it can be put into the hands of those who must execute it. George agreed: he would see that directions were sent out. Not a God-damned person must barge in in the mornings. Anything could be discussed later in the day. 'You're quite right. I'm the chief offender. You must be allowed to get on with your work.'

Thursday, 21 March

'He must not be disturbed.' The word went around. As a result, I drew like a fanatic. The hours went by in deep, uninterrupted pleasure. The sketches were better than those I did for the original Broadway production of the musical. It is not often that one gets a chance to use one's second thoughts.

I was surprised when lunchtime was presaged by the high voice of Gladys Cooper (our Mrs Higgins) next door. She had come to George's room with a pot of marmalade which she had made from the oranges grown in her garden, and a sheaf of early photographs of herself, taken at the time she was England's

1 'A scruffy sparrow'

2 Eliza Doolittle

3 'What's this for?'

4 & 5 Rex sings, 'I'm an ordinary man'

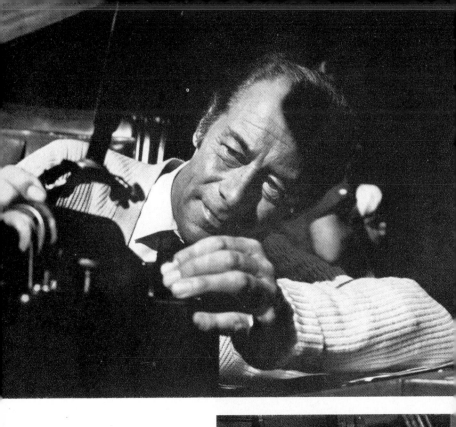

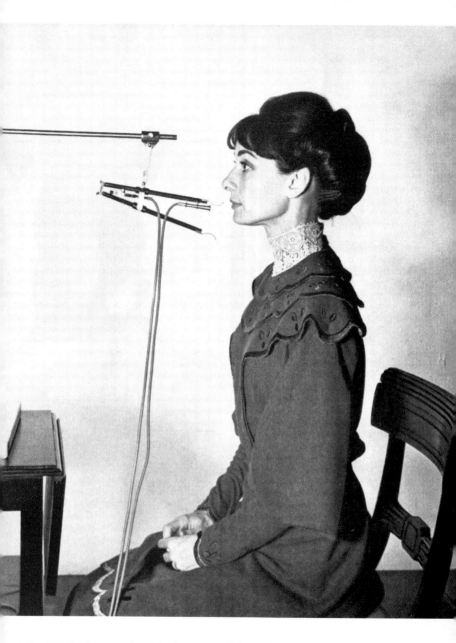

6 & 7 The Professor teaches Eliza how to speak beautifully

8 Four stages in Eliza's transformation

greatest beauty and the First Lady of the stage. These are to be used in connexion with a pre-Raphaelite portrait to be placed in Higgins' study.

Gladys has a marvellous way of facing the onslaught of the years. No excuses. Her eyes may have lost some of their lustre but none of their intensity. She does not give her past beauty a thought. She's too interested in everything else. She looks at you with seeing eyes. She breathes in fresh air. She radiates health, and her complexion is so burnt by the sun that it has become like a walnut. She told us what she eats. ('If you really want to know: hot water and lemon, first thing. Then a huge cup of milky coffee and prunes for breakfast. Only yogurt for lunch. And then I cook myself a proper meal for night.') She's Spartan and self disciplined, and she shamed me when talking of a portrait that Laszlo had painted for her in *The Admirable Crichton*, and I asked her if she had it with her out here. 'No, I told you the other night – you must have forgotten, or couldn't have been listening – a Maharaja bought it!' (Oh, the damage of the dry Martini!)

She talked with fervour of the *nouvelle vague* films and the new writers whose work was appearing in neighbourhood playhouses, and of fascinating details of the past. She quoted lines from forgotten plays, remembering every aspect of her career, and working with 'Pin' (Pinero), Maugham, Lonsdale, and her collaboration with the dress designer, Edward Molyneux ('He taught me about clothes.').

When complimented on her latest performance in a very bad moving picture, she said: 'Yes, I was driving in my Thunderbird and, suddenly, I had the idea to play the part like Constance Collier, very proud and authoritative. It's amazing how an idea can give you a clue to a whole character.'

I remembered the tremendous impression Gladys had made in a play with Paul Scofield when, after the last war, she came back to England. Her stage entrance was extremely poignant for she was playing a woman who, after a separation of twenty years, had come to help her son who was in some severe trouble. Gladys looked at him with such haunting sadness that the audience sat electrified. I asked her how she made this tremendous effect. 'What were you thinking about as you looked at him?' Gladys said: 'I always used to think "How extraordinary that you have grown so tall!" ' But pressed more to tell us her theories on her acting, she pooh-poohed. 'Oh, I don't think about it. After all these years, I just get out there and try to be heard and hurry through it as quickly as possible, and then go home.'

Although her loveliness made her the great picture post-card favourite and a household name throughout England, Gladys has never had the easy, pampered life of a famous beauty. Adulation, and tributes in the form of jewellery or flowers, have seldom come her way. At the height of her glory, her mother came to her dressing-room and said: 'You're too thin, dear! You're all nose!' She laughs wryly when today people ask her: 'Why haven't you retired?'

Friday, 22 March

Saw the first model for Higgins' house. This has taken much thought and time but, thanks to the visit of George and Gene to Dr Gottfried's rooms in Wimpole Street, we have been able to produce something that is unusual.

George's head appeared round the door. 'If we show all the servants in the Higgins' house, what are the sort of things some of them might be doing in the afternoon?' I scratched my head and suggested the following:

A kitchen-maid with a face like a codfish decorating with radishes and cucumber a large cold salmon.

A tweeny waving a footman's hair or moustache with hot curling tongs.

Tea and crumpets in bedroom-sitting room for Mrs Pearce and gossiping friend.

A housemaid trimming a hat with a duck's wing for her afternoon out.

For someone like myself, so completely unattuned to the machine age, there is much in Hollywood that baffles me. It was somewhat surprising when the carburettor of my car needed slight re-adjustment that the car was sent to the repair shop and simply replaced with a bigger and later one. When I explained that only a slight dickering was necessary they said, 'It's easier to give you a new one.' Three times my motor car has been changed. I now possess next year's model.

When I asked for a bottle of ink for filling my fountain pens, 'Ink! We don't use ink here any more,' an old hand at the studio told me. This news saddened me as I am allergic to ball points.

Again when I asked this same person to mail some private letters written on hotel paper she suggested re-addressing them on Warner's stationery. I protested. She produced a clipping from a local journal warning us that, in future, all envelopes must measure at least 3 by 4½ inches otherwise they would get caught in the machines.

Most baffling of all was when I received several small cheques in payment of my weekly salary. My agent was equally non-plussed. Eventually the Accounts Department explained that the IBM machine had been giving them trouble and they'd had to use other machines to rectify its mistakes. Oh, for the days of the Abacus!

Monday, 25 March

In the workrooms, a row of *toiles* of the Ascot costumes were on stands for my inspection and criticism. They left nothing to be desired. Hundreds of yards of materials and trimmings were chosen, and forthwith ordered, and the enthusiasm of Anne Laune and her staff was infectious. When creating the original production in New York, it was impossible to discover a shoe-maker who could provide us with ladies' slippers with pointed toes. Likewise, it was difficult to explain that bodices of evening dresses should not necessarily look like jewelled brassières. Fashion and the Empire line have caught up with us, and make life here much easier.

Tuesday, 26 March

Delighted at waking in my new Bel-Air surroundings. The octagonal ceiling seemed positively Palladian. George Hopkins has built me three huge bulletin boards on to which I will pin clippings and favourite pictures. When all the green plants arrive from 'Flowerland', the room will look like my own. From the patio came the sound of trickling water and the smell of jasmine. The marguerite bushes were covered with dew. This may be an artificial Arcadia, but it soothes and suffices.

Wednesday, 27 March

Pressure. George noticed my restlessness. 'Sit down, relax, perturbed spirit. What's the hurry?' It is difficult to define it: it was certainly self-inflicted activity, but there are certain mental processes which set themselves in motion and which must be obeyed. I felt that I'd been here long enough to have more put down on paper. Also, the Wardrobe is waiting, and I do not wish to find myself in the predicament of having to design during the inevitable last-minute rush.

Madame Przeworska was a brilliant dressmaker in London during the war years. She is now living in Los Angeles, and with her Hungarian husband, named Holt, has created an extraordinary collection of costumes of all periods at the Los Angeles Museum. Today, Anne Laune, Eleanor Abbey and myself visited Mrs Holt, who showed us Elizabethan embroideries and eighteenth-century brocades. But we were particularly interested in the 1913 fashions. It was valuable to us to be able to handle these dresses and learn so much about their ingenious composition. The greatest surprise was to find that often they were asymmetrical in cut, with trains that had not even two sides alike. Some of the creations were real works of art – audacious, strange and wild in their colour combinations – the cut so bold, so simple and elaborate of detail. Lucille, Callot, Cheruit, Poiret – their talent is still valid today. My childhood was evoked by the soft touch of the materials and the slightly sulphuric smell of the metallic embroidery and bead work. We were told that any of our cutters could come here and copy these dresses. We will certainly avail ourselves of this helpful offer.

The Hollywood traffic on the way to the studio has become so erratic that I decided that if once I became accustomed to the furious speed of the freeway, time and possible anxiety could be spared.

Two good friends, Jack Larson and Jim Bridges, volunteered to teach me the quick way from Bel-Air to Burbank and back. I delayed them in my octagonal room as I drank gin and tonic in order to acquire Dutch courage before they guided me on this journey.

For the past days I seem to have been collecting horror stories of the freeway: how novices found themselves in one lane, and since fellow motorists seldom allowed them to change into another, were not able to turn off for a hundred miles. The 'slow' traffic should remain in the right lane, but you could be given a ticket for holding up the flow of traffic. Sometimes the general speed of the onrush is such that the sudden breakdown of one automobile can cause a collision consisting of a seventy car pile-up.

Anyhow, here's trying! We drove along Sunset Boulevard at quite a normal pace watching the ever-increasing signs for the Sepulveda Freeway. 'Now, sharp turn right – a stop sign. Now quick! Now, beyond that roundabout, that's it. You have to turn left and go up the ramp. But make it fast! You mustn't hold things up!' As if we were about to take off into the air the Chevrolet mounted a ramp at flashing speed. Suddenly, we were on the freeway – golly!

The night, in the form of blinding, dazzling headlights, was rushing at one in every direction. No matter where one looked – in the mirror above one's head – or to the sides – meteors were in orbit everywhere. I had no idea where we were going, or where I was going, but I knew we were going somewhere pretty quick. Jack and Jim tried to be encouraging. 'Keep your foot pressed down hard. Keep going in the right lane because in five miles you're going to turn off for the Hollywood Freeway. Keep going fast. Nothing to worry about.'

But, in spite of the gin and tonic, I *did* worry. What if we were to have a flat tyre? Suppose the petrol ran out? Only recently, a married couple was speeding in a Cadillac when, suddenly, the steering went. The car flew off the road, crashed down a steep hill, hurtled through a garden fence and made straight for a swimming-pool where it sank in the deep end. Even while undergoing this series of shocks, the wife had the presence of mind to unwind the car window and, before she knew it, was floating to the top of the pool. The appalled owners of the swimming-pool rushed out of their house too late to extricate the husband, trapped under water with his head poking out of one of the half-opened windows. It adds horror to think that one cannot take to the highway without the possibility of a dip.

Somehow or other I managed the journey from Sunset Boulevard to Barham Boulevard and back three times in succession.

But having to drive solo on the freeway this morning was a different matter! Jack and Jim had written out my itinerary quite carefully. First I would go to the garage to have the tyres checked and the petrol tank filled. Then I must go up the ramp and on to the freeway, but not slowly – that was dangerous. I must join the general rush in a flash. Once on the immaculate strip of four lanes of wildly-rushing cars, my eyes were popping, not daring to look left or right. These great white ways stretch from San Diego, in the south, to San Francisco in the north with turns to the east that take one across the entire continent. What if I got into the wrong lane and couldn't stop between Bakersfield or New York? From what I could see of the occupants of other cars they seemed quite calm. One young man was even smoking non-chalantly, with cigarette held high, and only one hand on the wheel. One van was full of children with their legs hanging out of the windows. Surely it was a risk to bring so many young lives into this danger zone? Old rickety vans, piled high with swaying rubbish, and little tin Lizzies, buckled and bent, tore along, overtaking open sports cars. Old family barouches were filled with pets. A truckload of cardboard boxes was spilling its contents in the line of fire. Cars screamed to a halt, but my brakes were good. At one point in the road there appeared to be, in the path of on-rushing cars, a truncated hand. Perhaps, after all, it was only the rubber glove left by a workman. Most terrifying of all was the streak of lightning which passed in the shape of a vehicle filled with nuns. No doubt it was driven by the Mother Superior.

After a rather tough day's work in the studio, I was in no mood to take the freeway home, but take it I must: even if I croaked in the attempt.

The return journey was a Kafka-esque experience. The traffic roared towards a beautiful sunset of red and pink against blue mountains. The sun was so low that one could not read the signposts hanging above. Suddenly all the traffic came to a screeching halt. Ten thousand red car lights flashed in front. Thus, for an hour, we all remained almost stationary. A breakdown had caused the standstill. However, when the lanes opened up again, the flood had added speed and impatience, and hope seemed small of ever getting off into the left or right lanes. Before I could turn off I knew I was wrong to be heading towards Magnolia. Three times I had to get off the freeway, and three times to find my way back on again. My nightmarish misery lasted late into the night.

To design fifty new costumes for Ascot or the Ball is no problem, but at this point in the operations it often takes considerable time to devise just the right costume for a principal in a certain scene.

I showed George the designs for Gladys Cooper's costumes. We have decided not to make Mrs Higgins into the conventional Mrs Rittenhouse – Marx Brothers' dowager, but into quite an 'original', a Fabian, rather an aesthetic intellectual (for, after all, she is the mother of the young Bernard Shaw). To suggest the character is quite a tricky technical problem.

I wrote to Diana Cooper, asking what her mother, the Duchess of Rutland, would have worn at Ascot. The Duchess was an aesthetically-inclined beauty and a member of the 'Souls'. She dressed in a picturesque manner. Diana wrote: 'Certainly *cream*. A straw hat trimmed, of course, by herself, with little bits of bird's breast and/or ribbon in dirty pink, wide-ish brimmed and fairly shallow because of the Grecian back-handle, and the Sarah B. fringe in front. I don't suppose she ever set foot in a milliner's shop.

She would have been dressed from the old clothes cupboard with cream skirt to the ground, and cream shirt, and lace scarves around the neck held with paste brooches, a tortoise in enamel, and a bay leaf. The whole rag-bag camouflaged over by a *démodé*, once good, three-quarter length coat of beige, lace or brocade, inherited from sister Marjorie, perhaps. Good suede gloves (beige and long). Very high-heeled shoes she hoped didn't show. Parasol, of course.'

George's reaction to the sketches was positive and constructive. He said: 'You've gone way-out on the first one. We shouldn't see her as a freak: we must realize, by degrees, that she is intelligent, a woman of character. You've made her too altogether arty. Gladys must look lovely.'

The first tests were to be made of the various grey materials, to be ordered by the mile, for the men at Ascot, plus various other samples of tricky, in-between colours. Harry Stradling, the camera man, was most meticulous with his various lenses and meters. This is a highly technical business that takes time and more patience than I could ever summon up.

The tempo on the stage while the crew stood around waiting was somewhat *andante*, so I soon made an excuse to quit for the '*brio*' of Ladies' Wardrobe where Leah Barnes, the milliner, is a symphony of vitality. She has the face of an early Dutch or German Madonna, with a Texan Ruth Gordon's voice, and invariably puts on a series of the most outrageous Ascot hats, to which she somehow gives a Parisian style. Her uncurbed enthusiasm makes it a joy to work with her and, apart from her flair, she is a consummate technician.

I have infinite respect for the sometimes elderly women who, geared to the meticulousness of their craft, arrive early in the morning and who work throughout the long days with their diagrams and pieces cut out on paper – mere geometry to me – which mean that not an inch of material is wasted. Their precision and conscientiousness is miraculous. Sometimes, if I have designed a costume carelessly, they are forced to spend hours trying to find a solution.

Everyone is dedicated, calm and serene, and there is a refreshing quiet in the workroom.

The Wardrobe seems to have put on a spurt. Of the finished Covent Garden cloaks, some are like birds of paradise or Chinese pheasants. There is one in black, green and gold brocade, with ostrich feathers, that has all the grandeur of a Spanish funeral.

This is, from a costume point of view, a play about three women – Eliza, Mrs Higgins and Mrs Eynsford-Hill. They are surrounded by people who are all dressed as important characters. In this production there are virtually no 'extras' and, with the exception of the tails at the Ball, and the grey frock-coats at Ascot, there are no 'repeats'. Even the men in the cockney scenes are being created as individual characters, whose prototypes are to be found in Phil May, Belcher or photographs of the period. Among the four hundred women at the Ball and at Ascot, there is not one costume that has not been specially designed, or re-created from museum sources, with the care and attention given to a principal's clothes.

The sets, however, seem to take forever. The drawings for the builders are now being made in the Art Department from the two models that were finished two weeks ago. The amount of detail is prodigious, and I am impatient, for one always has the feeling of the ever-oncoming typhoon. We must finish as many sets as possible before the roar starts, for then it is a whole-time job to hold on to one's hat.

A telephone call from Stanley Holloway in London: should he have 'doubles' for his clothes? Yes, two sets of everything, for he has to be out in the rain and get thrown about on the way to his wedding.

A call to Rex Harrison in New York. 'Hold on, old chap, while I look inside my shoes for Tuczek's address. 18 Clifford Street . . . Hold on, while I look inside my coat to see if it has an address.' Sounds of laughter in the background. I am sending him one of my Locke hats to try on, as I want to influence him to change from the former hat, which has become too well known in every small city throughout this country.

Racing along the almost deserted freeway, I wondered at the shortness of time that it takes to become accustomed to terror. Only a few mornings ago I would arrive at the studio tingling with nervous exhaustion after the hazards of the trip. But now it seems natural to be roaring along as part of a four-lane stream with the screams and 'whooshes' of the oncoming traffic only divided from one by a wire fence. The noise itself is frightening.

The roar drowns out the airplanes and the helicopters, but occasionally one passes in between two trucks that rumble with the *basso* thunder of hell, while, above the general din, a racing motorist splits the ear revving his engine with the shriek of the tearing of a vast canvas sheet.

Today, the placing of furniture in Higgins' house was discussed, so that Hermes Pan, the choreographer, will know where his dance movements can run.

If I were to keep up this diary only on weekends instead of making these tedious jottings early each morning, I would be hard put to remember one day from another. A Wednesday or Thursday at the studio is differentiated only by a mood or some remark. Yet the weeks are never monotonous. It is like being in a play of a year's run. Each performance has its own individual life. Always present is the element of the unexpected. Sometimes the shocks are unaccountable, and not always healthy.

Wednesday, 17 April

Only an Englishman would bathe in this early morning fog. But, since no one ever walks in Hollywood, this is my one source of exercise. After splashing about a bit I sat by the pool, teeth chattering, reading letters from home. One from my gardener, Smallpeice, said, 'In the Winter Garden there is an abundance of jasmine again, and with the last bowls of hyacinths out the scent in there is delightful. On the table I have got pots of the silver leaf Echeveria which I believe you like very much with its spikes of pink bells. Mr Porte has made a successful job of fixing the small water pump, and we now have a continuous supply of running water in the pond again'.

Friday, 3 May

In the Art Department we talked about a colour chart for painting Covent Garden market. Get rid of black. Use muted greens and lilacs among the grey and buff bits. I showed, as a guide, an oil sketch that I'd just done, and which was well received by Gene and Ed, the illustrator, but George Cukor was of the opinion that the camera would pick up every colour with such force that it would be safest to play for monochrome.

Back in Wardrobe, where seventy women, having progressed from Covent Garden to the magpies of Ascot, are now starting on opal-coloured costumes of the Ball scene.

'Anyone want to see me?' 'No, not today,' smiled Barbara. Louise and Lucia, too, were engrossed in their work, so I stopped to confer with Agnes Koschin, who was born in Siberia, escaped with her husband from Russia three years after the revolution, to live seventeen years in China before coming to California.

Although much too young to have lived in it, she has a remarkable instinct for the period we are re-creating.

Occasionally we have a bad day, and some dresses are a disappointment. We battle against odds. However, the average is high. The 'feel' of this production is different from the stage.

All in their own ways, the fitters have their excellences. Louise, like Mother Earth, is a fine tailor. Carol, so pretty, with her grey hair and star eyes, must have been too beautiful to need talent as a young girl, yet had developed a great sense of design and knows instinctively when something is lacking. Lucia, who is Italian, is past-mistress at manoeuvring frothy, light lace. Barbara looks worried and persevering, but she knows her *métier* as well as any. Helen, a handsome Duchess with white hair, is terribly nervous with me, but need not be because I'm delighted with everything she does. Mr Morris is a sentimental little owl, and his voice is so packed with emotion that he seems as if he is weeping. 'Oh, I like to work on that. It's a pleasure!' he beams unctuously. 'I don't want to put any fur on it. It's far better as it is.' The tailoring of his coats is impeccable. His latest creation is a silver cape that Helen wore with such pride and shyness. Everyone complimented her on her appearance. 'If only I were young!' she said.

An Italian, Filamina, with her spectacles worn on her head, the better to give unhindered winks, is full of sly fun.

Most of the laughs are to be found in the millinery corner. One hat looks like a weather-vane on which half a dozen crows are trying to alight: another is a large chauffeur's cap made of most unsuitable materials, while yet another is just an upturned bucket with a cascade of ostrich feathers. The work girls take off their spectacles and pose in the most outrageous millinery. But this is not merely a fun-fair. These are great artisans whose craft is apparent in so many delicate nuances of understanding and experience. If these hats were made by a heavy hand, they would be vulgar, ugly and impractical.

Leah's enthusiasms come from doing something that is, perhaps, the best she has ever done. 'Oh, this makes me flip,' she says, as she puts on a Gothic monster of black spikes. This is a *tour de force* on her part, for she has fashioned it with the subtlety of a piece of modern sculpture. Recently my designs have become more and more 'difficult'. Yet, to date, they do not seem to be a stumbling block. To see the drawings and designs, made in a hurry two months ago, suddenly brought to fruition is a real thrill.

On Stage 2, Higgins' house is being built. It is a most intricate and ingenious arrangement with the three floors and their staircases built side by side on the sound stage instead of one above the other as in a real house. In spite of the difficulty of the staircases being cut off sharp, half-way up-or downstairs, it now begins to take shape. Many aspects of the transplanted house – the nodes and crannies – are so familiar to me that I feel that Dr Gottfried will materialize at any minute to give me an injection.

Now came the agreeable job of choosing wallpaper for the different rooms and corridors from a great parcel of strange 1910 designs that was flown from Coles in London this morning. Although Hollywood studios are perfectionists at reproducing any given thing it is often difficult to find the original to be copied.

Thursday the . . .?

On the way to the swimming-pool in the smog I saw, among the richly-thriving new species of day-glow coloured roses in the bed, a huge, coarse, blue delphinium. I could have spat at it. It brought about the realization that I was, like Ruth, amid the alien corn, sick for home.

Living as I am in the tarmac and plaster world of the Freeway and the Studio, there are no opportunities, except at occasional week-ends, of watching the passage of the year. It was to inhale the ozone, and to smell the herbs and wild flowers of the Northern coast of California several hundred miles away that I would take an airplane on some Friday evenings. There one regained the sense of being part of the world that one has missed here in this 'No Man's Land' of specious nature, synthetic 'loveliness' and ubiquitous 'clean comfort stations'.

That delphinium reminds me that, in England, this was the time of the year when I could hardly drag myself from my garden for fear of missing the opening of a bud. Of course, here it *would* grow as large as that! And at the same time as every other flower of the summer! Here, everything comes out within the same week. In England, the departure of winter is a long, drawn-out process, and how welcome is the first scylla and grape hyacinth! When the lilac is in blossom we feel spring upon us. We have to wait for high summer for a delphinium! But here it has no value, because it grows too readily when everything else is available. Nothing is rare except quality.

This afternoon the Director had his first glimpse of the costumes. I was worried, remembering so well how one day, when he was a fellow sufferer in another production, we had asked him to shut his eyes until Gladys Cooper would appear, dressed as his leading lady. We were so enthusiastic about her appearance that we expected eulogies. But George opened his eyes and said 'No! It's no good. She doesn't look as if she'd ever been rich!' Today, however, the story was different. His praises thrilled all in Wardrobe. Everyone laughed and made jokes. We were very happy. Joe Hiatt led the flattery. 'They have never made such clothes! They are all wild about what they are doing. But it is the man who has inspired them all. Cecil inspires confidence. And when have you seen a designer introduce each cutter to the Director?' George, determined to bring matters back to reality, said, 'Oh, I've met cutters before.'

However, whether he had met cutters or not, my mood, as I went off home, was one of euphoria: my Chevrolet, enhanced by a newly-equipped radio, tore along the freeway as my ears were filled with the soaring violins of gipsy love songs.

Rex Harrison has sent me a letter denigrating the hat I sent him as 'a Stetson type', and please not to order one like it as he looks ghastly in it. After many jokes about my not getting my own hat back, he has written: 'Good God! Well, I never dreamt that truly handsome, attractive, personality-hat was yours!'

Perhaps fatigue had prompted me to criticize one or two of Leah's new hats last evening more than I should. Today there was only praise. Praise, also, for the Men's Wardrobe boys, Geoff and Bob, who gave us our first inspection of the cockney clothes. They have succeeded in the impossible – of making them look real, and not like fancy dress.

Alan Lerner is here again, but is off to arrange a party for President Kennedy's birthday next week.

Thursday, 16 May

Alan was long overdue. When he turned up he was slightly on the defensive. 'You've been avoiding me!' he barked at me. But no one can take umbrage with Alan, for the minute he starts working the creative juices start to flow all around. Buck Hall, the assistant Director, had said that Alan's mind was as sharp as a steel trap. I had not heard this somewhat hackneyed simile before and thought it very apt. But Alan is, as usual, trying to fit in more than it is possible to do in his short stay. God knows what he didn't do during this morning.

But after lunch, we accompanied him to listen to a girl singing Eliza's songs, in case Audrey's voice proves to be too frail for one or two of the more operatic arias, and a few notes have to be dubbed. Then, having given advice on the dance routines, Alan saw the costumes and, at the sight of them, decided on a sudden switch for the beginning of the film. Instead of starting off with the poverty of Covent Garden, we would see the elegant Wagner-ites leaving the Opera, running through the market in a sudden squall, then working up to a great entrance for rain-sodden Eliza.

By now I take in my morning stride the frenetic Freeway journey to the studio. It is almost as automatic a procedure as washing one's teeth. But, once off the prescribed route, the business of finding one's way about Hollywood, especially in Beverly Hills at night, is fraught with hazards. With real estate of such in-flationary value, overcrowding becomes a word with new overtones, and it is not surprising that in order to possess a plot of ground with a view, and possibly a small lozenge of garden, some of even the most privileged live on the precipitous incline of a mountain that can be navigated with only the most powerful engine, the strongest of brakes, and fiercest determination. I have often turned my car, believing that to continue would be to court certain disaster, only to become aware that unflinchingly I should have ventured further.

In spite of the most minute written instructions, I have invari-ably the greatest trouble in finding, for the first time, any given address. How often have I burnt my fingers with matches looking, in the dark, for some non-existent signpost telling me of the whereabouts of 19990 Hidden Valley Road, Cold Canyon Drive! Added complications set in when the same winding drive in Beverly Hills is suddenly allocated to Los Angeles, so that the numbers of the houses, having reached to the nine thousands, suddenly switch to two hundred and thirteen. No cop appears to put you out of your predicament, and certainly no pedestrian materializes to collect a newspaper or letter from the mail boxes – for walking is something that does not happen here.

Hearing the woes of others it comforts me to discover that I am by no means alone in these quandaries, that even those who live here have match-burnt fingers, and that strong men and women have become almost hysterical losing themselves for three hours in an effort to get on or off a freeway.

Arriving late for dinner at the Kirk Douglas' tonight (I had mistaken N. Canon Drive for N. Camden Drive) I was in a hurry to park my car in front of number 707 before the last guests arrived. (I need not have worried – will I never learn that it is almost impossible ever to be late for a large Hollywood dinner-party?) On getting out of the car I realized I was not parked parallel enough to the curb. In again to back a bit. That would do it. I ran up the drive and into the celebrations where, of course, I enjoyed myself, mindless of tomorrow's early call.

When, at a late hour, I left the party, a strange and rather terrifying sight greeted me. Outside, near the curb of the road, an illumination display of flickering lights had been arrayed. To the height of twelve feet scarlet stars were swaying and blinking. By degrees my eyes descried in their midst a crimson automobile which was hanging upside down from a chain.

Suddenly I realized that the car was mine, and that they were doing something cruel and ignominious to my 'house on the road'. A lorry carrying a tall crane was about to tow away forever my faithful old bus which now hung in mid-air like a carcass of meat. Desperately I pleaded with the truck-driver. 'Can't I have my car back?' I moaned. 'Too late, buddy. It's in the hands of the police now.' 'If it's cash that's needed, how much do they want?' It seems that I backed the car so that it partly obstructed the garage entrance to the Douglas' neighbours. They had kindly telephoned the police to inform on my mis-demeanour. The Police Patrol had arrived, given me a ticket, and ordered the car to be taken to some incomprehensible address. 'Can't I come with you?' 'Better call a cab.' However, eventually I prevailed upon the truck-driver to let me into the front seat with him and progress through Beverly Hills with my upturned car rolling on two wheels behind. In his office at a vast, inhuman garage, the truck-driver spent the better part of an hour writing out the particulars and description of my motor car. His detailed examination done, he handed me a sheaf of papers: these I had to take to the Police Station. The emergency night squad, see-ing me in dinner jacket, no doubt expected to find a recalcitrant drunk. However, they were amused by my abject apologies, phrased in what, no doubt, seemed to them exaggeratedly English terms and they became particularly friendly. The dawn approached when they thanked me for my co-operation, allowed me to return to the garage and reclaim my long-lost friend from among the thousands of other abandoned cars, and, thirty-five dollars out of pocket and minus three hours' precious sleep, to drive it back home, on all four wheels.

Work this morning was to take place in Cukor's garden, where Alan would give us an outline for the new beginning of the picture. When I rang Alan from the swimming-pool at the hotel, we discovered we had rooms next to one another. He brightly and cheerfully said: 'I'll join you in the pool.' Luckily, I didn't wait. Half an hour after we were due at Cukor's, I went into Alan's room to find him lying on the bed in pyjamas, a telephone propped on his shoulder, talking to Fritz Loewe in Palm Springs. (Fritz, talking to me, said: 'Of course I'm not coming to Hollywood. Why should I? I'm already rich, and I'm famous'.) Alan also had calls from New York about the party for the President.

I preceded Alan, who arrived an hour later. At once he was extemporizing a whole new sequence for the first part of the film. He was inspired. 'Oh God!' he said at one point, seeing in front of him the endless amount of extra work he would have to do, 'all these ideas must be put on paper.' But, again, 'What the hell!' flashed through his mind. This was important! 'So here goes.' His 'steel-trap' was freshly plated.

Scenes were juggled about, but in the new form everything seemed to fit better. There was great improvement on the former treatment for introducing Doolittle, and for doing away with a reprise of 'With A Little Bit Of Luck'. 'What do we have during the overture, and for the titles?' asked Cukor. Looking at the garden bed in front of him, Alan said: 'I'd like flowers.' I saw myself enthusiastically planning a long panning shot of flowers in baskets, as in the market: thickly-packed country flowers, and spring flowers: peonies, lilacs, daises. These would gradually melt into the vivid patterns of the ladies' cloaks as they are leaving the foyer of the Opera, and over all these effects the 'credits' will be written.

Alan said: 'Do you know, a pansy is the only flower you can actually see open in front of your eyes? I was determined to watch one, so once I sat staring in front of me for eight hours with a bottle of champagne! Eventually the bloody thing opened. God-damn it, I'm crazy about flowers!'

From the new running order we progressed as far as Ascot, and here Alan had some good ideas: an affected lady, before the race, with a white-gloved hand, feeding her horse with lumps of sugar; the lady in my Poiretesque dress (with the design which looks like eyes all over it) could have a squint; Lady Boxington's hat should be so enormous that Eliza, to her added consternation, can never see her face; two ladies, blinded by the brims of their hats, must almost collide as they walk towards each other. But, at the point of contact, one brim passes under the other with only a quarter of an inch to spare. Rex Harrison's entrance to be marred by his stepping on some woman's train and ricocheting on to another, thereby knocking off her voluminous headgear.

In order to avoid a 'process-shot' of the return in the motor-car from Ascot, Mrs Higgins and her son should be discussing Eliza's shortcomings, oblivious of the shocked ladies who are staggering home, some even having to be supported or carried away on stretchers.

Jack Warner was on the telephone to tell George he had read in one session the finished script Alan has left behind him. Jack thought it so brilliant that he has decided he wants to be the sole Producer on the picture.

Saturday, 18 May

Our leading lady has arrived from Switzerland: George, Alan and I went to pay a formal call on Audrey Hepburn Ferrer at tea time. Sean, her two-year-old son, was present, and it is obvious that this is the love affair of her life, and she of her son's.

The rented house is large, white and cool, and is now inhabited by the entire Ferrer household, complete with Sean's plump and cosy Italian nanny. Two smiling girls served tea and home-made apricot jam roll.

Suddenly Audrey asked with absolute candour: 'Are you going to use my voice for songs at all?' This was disarming and removed any awkwardness in approaching a difficult subject since it might have been a disappointment to her if she learned (like Leslie Caron in *Gigi*) that some of her voice would be dubbed. It was now easy to say that, quite probably, Audrey's voice will be used for many of the songs, but certain notes might be interpolated from another voice. Audrey said: 'I'll understand if you do, but in any case I'll work hard on my voice, have as many lessons as you like. It's all part of the business, to learn to sing and dance.'

Audrey's enthusiasm was contagious. But I am more superstitious than I like to admit: it almost worried me when she said: 'This picture is one we must all remember. Wonderful talents, everyone right, everyone happy. It's the high spot, let's enjoy it!' Her mouth, her smile, her teeth, are delicious, the expression of her eyes melting. Her calm quality of purity and integrity is rare.

After lunch, Jack Warner came to make a tour of the sets. Warner's jokes became less prolific as his admiration mounted.

He said Covent Garden was the biggest set they'd built since early Errol Flynn days. His enthusiasm was welcome, for these sets, which rely less than most on the *trompe l'oeil* effects of paint, and are made of solid wood and plaster, have each cost almost a quarter of a million dollars. They are admittedly the biggest and heaviest we will need in the picture, yet the final bill is not likely to be less than eight hundred thousand dollars.

Audrey and her husband, Mel, came to my room. Audrey wore a white felt pudding basin on the back of her head and looked like a tired child. She and Mel each sat with a book of my sketches on their laps, and suddenly Mel held up a sketch of Eliza as the flower girl. 'Look at that, Audrey! That's got it all. That's what it's all about. Oh, Audrey, it's just what you needed!' Audrey closed her eyes and smiled like a Bisto kid. 'Oh, it's more than I thought it possibly could be. It's too much!' Such genuine enthusiasm thrilled me, particularly since that sketch represented quite a concentrated effort to create the outward appearance of Audrey's interpretation of the cockney. When others had looked at it, they had busily talked about some other subject: I had been more discouraged than I realized. I now felt the air was filled with oxygen.

Audrey and Mel came with me to Wardrobe where they gasped at the first things they saw, and these were not the most interesting. The combination of Audrey and these exaggerated clothes created comic magic. She wanted to pose for photographs in every one of them. 'I don't want to play Eliza! She doesn't have enough pretty clothes. I want to parade in all these.' And she did: they will never look so well on anybody else. She was adorable in the Romney big-brimmed hats and the tea cosies and Gaby Deslys caps, tricorns, bicorns, pudding-basins, mob-caps, Bretons, cartwheels and Frans Hals' cavalier hats. She gave added contrast to black velvet and white lace, extra charm to broderie anglaise and to taffeta ribbons, apotheosized muslin and satin.

Eleanor Abbey has found, in her casual but clever way, among a collection of old clothes some oddly assorted garments that vaguely resemble the rough, pencilled suggestions I gave her. These she has re-cut and pinned together to create a poignant first appearance for Eliza. Tacked on to a dummy stand, the effigy beguiled by its pathos everyone who looked at it; it was more successful than anything one could have rigidly designed. When Audrey saw Eliza's thin green coat, drab skirts and black boater, she was so moved by compassion that she gulped – like a fish out of water. Later, when she put on Eliza's blouses and skirts for the lessons in how to become a lady, it was one's own heart that was touched.

Early fittings, with Audrey in a gay mood, making rubber faces, speaking in Eliza's cockney accent, joking with all the adoring helpers.

Tuesday, 4 June

Gene came into my office to talk about the Ascot sets. A great deal of time was spent trying to find even the roughest solution. However, I feel the whole sequence can be fresh and startling only if it is stylized, but not if we have to see the race track itself or a view of the great crowds.

Later Gene and I went to Stage Seven to see Covent Garden nearing completion. St Paul's Church has become a thing of poetry, painted in half-impressionistic manner; but the realism is such that I couldn't believe that this church was built today and not in 1633, or that scene painters, and not ninety thousand pigeons, had been spattering the stonework of Inigo Jones's lofty columns.

A Press luncheon for *My Fair Lady* was held on one of the stages of the studio to which thirty photographers and many journalists were invited. A long table was placed on a dais, decorated by Chasens with the taste that permitted the inclusion, among the sweet-peas, of those abominations of today – plastic flowers. The photographers were brutal. One man shouted at Cukor: 'Get back! You leant forward and covered Rex Harrison!' George, quite rightly furious, bellowed back: 'Who are you?' I suffered the greatest humiliation with poor grace, and loathed the whole proceedings with such hatred that only Gladys Cooper could calm me by quoting Dion Boucicault: 'Don't sink into the mud with them.' Max Bercutt and his Press Department all looked worried. Little wonder! The journalists asked some pretty impertinent questions about the costs of the production, but Jack Warner, the genius of business that he undoubtedly is, remained smiling. He made a speech and railed against the criticisms levelled at Hollywood. 'Hollywood is not on the rocks. It is anything but finished. We've got a bigger programme planned here than for many years! But we are not going to sully ourselves with the dirt of the pictures made in Spain, France or Italy. This industry is flourishing, and we can make just as good atmosphere pictures on the lot here as in Siberia or England.'

Audrey managed to look calm throughout. She and Hedda Hopper were the stars. Hopper looks like an elegant French hostess of the eighteenth century. She isn't, but I can't help admiring her gall.

Am reading Chekhov's letters: 'The truly gifted always remain in obscurity, avoid the crowd, and shun as much as possible the display of their talents ... An empty barrel makes more noise than a full one.'

A singing voice invited me to 'Come on in and see my secrets'. It was Audrey in the Makeup Department. 'Now, you see, I have no eyes!' Without the usual mascara and shadow, however, Audrey's eyes are like those in a Flemish painting and are even more appealing – young and sad. Yet it was extraordinary to see that it is simply by painting her eyes she has become a beauty in the modern sense. But having seen her without these aids, I will try to prevail upon her to do away with them in the earlier sequences, for this will give an entirely new and authentic look.

Later came the vital job of turning Audrey into Eliza by doing her hair. This is always one of the trickiest sessions, for the star is hyper-sensitive, hairdressers are, at best, the least easy of people, and opinions are expressed on all sides. One has to be firm about things one knows little about from the practical point of view, yet must stick to the picture in one's mind's eye. Eventually Audrey, in Eliza's black straw flower-girl hat, looked much the way I had hoped: a different appearance from any we have seen before in her pictures.

Audrey brought me a bunch of roses from her garden with a note of thanks for the photographs which I had taken of her wearing the extra-girls' dresses, which read: 'Dearest C.B.: Ever since I can remember I have always so badly wanted to be beautiful. Looking at those photographs last night I saw that, for a short time at least, I am, all because of you. Audrey.' ♡

Audrey was relieved that the first reading with Rex and Stanley Holloway had gone well this afternoon. She had been as nervous as when she first sang for the assembled company. 'But the others had all the values right, and I'm such a newcomer I felt I was drowning.'

Tuesday, 11 June

Today's prop and furniture hunt in spite of the tropical heat was more productive than any of the former ones. George Hopkins took me to a furnace where they specialize in 'impossible' furniture. We bought extraordinary washstands, complete with every sort of receptacle, unlikely tables from India and China; peacocks in majolica, and a multitude of things that reminded me of my first home: biscuit and cigar containers that my father kept in the billiard room, a huge carved dog's head made as a letter rack, silver pheasants with removable necks, and many such fantasies for the Professor's study. It was like being married to Higgins to choose the contents of his house, knowing his taste and recognizing the various curious objects and pictures that would go in different rooms.

Rehearsals are taking place in Higgins' house. Rex, strangely enough, was having difficulty with his lines after at least five years in the part. Audrey was already very touching and real.

I started to design Audrey's last act dress, but when George saw the sketch he suggested something more waspish and stylish. I thought a lyric note was needed. Now I must think again. *Later*: I can't think of anything that suits the mood.

If an additional costume is suddenly asked for, I cast my mind back to the days at Temple Court, when adult life was opening to me as a wonder and a revelation.

By trying to re-create some excitement that has survived my adolescence so many years ago, there is more likelihood of an impact being made upon today's spectator than if I were to search for a new inspiration among the old periodicals of the period. The reasons why Eliza Doolittle and other characters wear certain clothes are known only to me. Sometimes I am amused to think of relations and long-lost childhood friends turning up on the Warner's lot. But it is astonishing how a certain colour combination and a contrast of materials, that delighted me so long ago, still holds its validity today.

Monday, 17 June

Jim McGuire was with me on the floor of my room, and once again we were choosing doorknobs, handles and locks for the Higgins' drawing-room, study and the maids' bedrooms. These items are, perhaps, unimportant but, none the less, have to be done, and they take a great deal of time. 'What are you doing in Hollywood?' 'Choosing door furniture.'

After a long rehearsal Audrey was still as fresh as a flower for her dress fittings. She agrees the Los Angeles Museum dress is in the mood for Eliza's return to Covent Garden. We will make the neckline of *point d'esprit* cut from an old parasol. It will have the authentic touch.

Tuesday, 18 June

Rex spent the morning fitting his wardrobe. Joe Hiatt was so anxious to please him that he suggested having Rex's work-a-day trousers pressed during the fitting. Where else could you get such service?

Rex was in a good mood and thoroughly approved of his first suit, eulogized his cape-coat and conceded that the new, slightly larger-brimmed hat was an improvement. The Men's Wardrobe could hardly believe their ears as suit after suit was pronounced equally successful. Rex even accepted with alacrity the Norfolk jacket. We all went off to lunch in a state of jubilation.

Wednesday, 19 June

Sometimes a good deal of time is spent deciding whether one particular kind of beading for a dress is better than another: very likely the dress in question will never be seen on screen, but once one gives up and becomes careless the rot sets in. Besides, I wouldn't be able to look Louise straight in the eye.

This afternoon, however, Eliza's ball dress was pinned, in rough form, on a stand for the first time. This is a dress that everyone will see. Agnes has the responsibility of creating this gossamer shift. She started to cut the sequin, crystal and chenille embroidery from a genuine 1910 evening gown which will be an invaluable guide for our embroideries. Absorbed in such fascinating detail, I didn't realize the day was long since over, yet none of the women seemed in a hurry to get back to their homes.

Thursday, 20 June

Alan came in to say goodbye before he flies to New York. He will return in two weeks, meanwhile leaving a train of brilliant ideas in his path.

Tests are long-drawn-out, hapless affairs. Tests were again made today of the progress of Eliza's tuition period. I stand over Audrey like a Svengali, ordering strands of her hair to be placed in this direction or that, suggesting more or less eyelash, selecting a brooch or a trinket. At last she is ready to be seen by the Director and, if he approves, she is submitted to the even more relentless scrutiny of Harry's camera. At the end of one test, and after Audrey had been photographed by the still men for Wardrobe reference, she asked me if I would care to take a snap of her. After three minutes in front of my Rolleiflex Audrey went off to prepare for the next change: she would send for me when she was ready for me to come and stage-manage proceedings.

Meanwhile George sent for Max Bercutt, head of Publicity, who passed on the information that I was not to take any pictures of Audrey during her tests, as it made Mr Cukor nervous. It was, perhaps, wiser that I should confide my almost uncontrollable fury and sense of frustration to George's emissary rather than beard Caesar himself, for my emotions were deeply roused.

Yesterday's scene continues to rankle for now I see clearly that I am being used as a sort of I.B.M. machine – the sort that does not break down – regardless of my personal reactions. When making a moving picture of this scale the burden of responsibility upon the Director, however old a hand he may be at the game, is heavy, but there are still three weeks before shooting starts – and it will be tough going if the strain has started to show already, or worse, if there has developed what Irving Lazar, our mutual agent, has called a 'clash of temperament'.

Friday, 21 June

I asked Buck Hall and Petch if everything is all right. 'Is anything all right?' they answered.

Saturday, 22 June

Audrey's thinness came from starvation during and after the war, her mother told me. They had gone on a visit to Holland and found themselves trapped. When, at last, they were able to leave for England, one and four pence worth of meat was the ration per person a week. Since they were unable to get at their money they almost starved.

At this time Audrey was not only practising ballet but appearing in cabarets and at performances at school. Then she was in the chorus of *High Button Shoes*. At one time, she was doing as many as twenty-eight performances a week. With Audrey today being paid a star's salary, it's extraordinary to think of the changes that have taken place in twenty-five years.

Sunday, 23 June

The summer season is upon us, and the hotel pool-life has started. A crowd of people appear and frequent the snack bar for hamburgers and ice-cream: to cap the canned music relayed from the hall, someone in a neighbouring patio is playing, at full volume, a commentary on a golf tournament. As it's a sports event, no one complains.

Monday, 24 June

Among the mountains and valleys of material almost submerging Miss Betty Huff and her stock-room in 'Wardrobe', it is soothing to choose colours and textures; it is satisfying, too, when one can change things that have gone wrong: Gladys Cooper's Ascot dress, for instance. We discovered we had done everything back to front, using materials inside that should have been outside. We will now proceed differently under the auspices of Agnes, and I know that when she is around we need not despair.

As I left Wardrobe, at the end of the day, I passed down the corridors of glassed-in cases where so many of the best costumes from past film productions are stored. What enthusiasm, what work went into the making of all these elaborate garments! A whole history of picture-making was represented by these braided, buttoned, embroidered vests, tunics and skirts: nuns' habits, Charles II courtiers, 1914 war uniforms, cowboys, Spanish, Russian and Mexican dancers: Bette Davis – Elizabethan and Marie Antoinette (Lana Turner style). The wardrobes of Grace Moore, Clark Gable, Errol Flynn and James Dean remind us of life's short span. The thought struck me that in the not too far future the dresses we are embarking upon with such zest will also take their place along these rows.

Twelve Hollywood extras dressed to look like cockneys struck no chord of recognition in me. With pallid, foetus faces they stood to attention, obviously with the curse of sterility upon them, and eyed everyone who scrutinized them with a mixture of insolence and pride. They looked like 'so much nothing', as my Aunt Jessie used to say. Joe Hiatt said it was the first time he'd seen clothes look better on racks than on people. They lacked precisely that very gristle of poverty and strength which I had seen in the real Covent Garden. When the unhappy band were brought before Cukor for judgement, he scourged them, saying to Buck Hall, 'Go on searching! Get people who have character and individuality.' Everyone was upset. Luckily I was spared the full scene, as Gene Allen and I had an important meeting, sitting on the steps of a dressing-room on Stage 7 while we scrutinized the preliminary blueprints for the Ascot scenes. The sun poured down on to our papers; gusts of wind contorted them before they were firmly held beneath our feet.

After half an hour's intense and uninterrupted concentration, the two of us were satisfied. We had decided on something which I think will be quite stylish in its simplicity.

Tuesday, 25 June

After all this time, there is a last-minute rush to get floor-plans so that Cukor can rehearse the entire picture. This suits me fine.

At her entrance, the Queen of Transylvania must be a personage of enormous authority. On an inspiration Cukor telephoned to

Fritzi Massary, the comic opera star from Berlin and Vienna, who is now living in retirement in Beverly Hills. Lubitsch had said of her that she was the greatest living performer, and her fame, as the original 'Dollar Princess' and 'Madame Pompadour', is legendary. When Cukor asked her to play the part of the Queen, she laughed uproariously. 'How do you know I won't die? I'm eighty-one, and I'll be gone before the picture starts! Does she have a lot to say? Ha! Ha! Ha! It's a great joke! I must tell Lisl, my daughter!'

In came the eighty-one-year-old Fritzi Massary, well-dressed, shod and gloved. She wore a raffish hat with a veil. She looked fifty-five. Petite, and thin to the point of reminding one of an ortolan, she proved conclusively that giants still tread the earth. Fritzi has the grand manner for all time, and is today as impressive as the great star of forty years ago.

Yes, she admits she *is* lonely. As Voltaire said, 'When one is old one plays cards'. She does. And reads with deep absorption. Or swims and takes her dog for a walk. Luckily, she is busy writing her life, which Lisl may publish, if she wishes, after her death. She said she had had a good share of life – success, work, and tragedy too: she had lost a husband and a country. Once the toast of Berlin, she was denounced by Hitler, but on her eightieth birthday she returned to Berlin to receive the keys of the city. Those that had scorned her before asked, 'Can you ever forgive?' To which she replied, 'Yes, but I can never forget'.

Fritzi is vastly entertained at the idea of playing the Queen of Transylvania, for, she says, all her friends are so thrilled. But wagging a finger at George, she rasped: 'Money! Let's talk about the money!' Her diamond pin flickering, she laughed: 'Who will I get in touch with about the business end? Because I will be very expensive!'

Wardrobe is continually visited by famous stars who create little impression on the workers. But today's visitor, although her name was unknown to them, was obviously an exception. Everyone watched this little figure, with the distinguished line and dignity of movement, place her pointed feet with that grace and sense of self-preservation that is only acquired by actresses accustomed to the dark mysteries of backstage, or by Royalty. Everyone responded to her wit, gusto, and reverence for tradition; they recognized the sense of humanity that emanates from greatness. Fritzi, famous for the perfection of her stage clothes, glowed when shown the sketch for her ball gown. After her miniscule measurements had been taken, she was driven happily away from the heat of the studio.

Because half-a-dozen people wanted me at the same time, I felt hounded. Gene appeared with a rough draft of a portrait of Gladys Cooper, done in pre-Raphaelite style, for correction. 'Make the dove a lily. Make the hair fuller. Paint the whole thing

more meticulously – less impressionistic.' He showed me some blueprints for the Embassy staircase. 'Make the tops of the panels semicircular – not squashed.' Bob Richards arrived from Men's Wardrobe with samples for Rex's dressing-gown and pyjamas. He said: 'Do you think, as Rex sweats so much, two pyjamas are enough?' Joe about artificial flowers from Paris being mistaken by Customs for real and consequently being impounded: Jim about more doorknobs, and Robbie about a prop handkerchief for wiping Audrey's nose. A decision: 'no' to the swans on Eliza's bedpost, but 'yes' to having the cretonne curtains of the same design as the wallpaper behind the bedhead. George Hopkins told me he has bought this silver bed from a woman who had asked $20,000 for the pair, but accepted $700 for one.

Audrey, herself, was waiting for me to direct the various hairstyles she should wear in the interim stages between being the Cockney flower seller and the resplendent butterfly. Tough going. Eventually, we achieved several effects that were completely authentic, rather stiff, with Gertie Millar bangs. To me they were delightful, as well as amusing and certainly different, but it would take someone as intelligent as Audrey to try something so far removed from today's accepted idea of prettiness.

Wednesday

I no longer lunch in George's room.

Thursday, 27 June

Audrey spent her time being tested for make-ups and hairstyles although she didn't feel well. The cruel motion-picture camera shows so much that is invisible to the naked eye. Tests were made with no make-up, with a pale, opalescent foundation, then a strong make-up, with lips, without lips, with dirt, without dirt, and hair matted and covered with dust. All the time people were pulling at her hair, her hat, smearing her face with paint, Audrey showed enormous understanding, tact and a willingness to learn. The hour of the lunch break was devoted by her to having her voice trained. Having worked on it like a Trojan ever since her arrival, her voice has improved to such an extent that she will be singing most of Eliza's songs. After lunch she wore the dresses which, we presume, Mrs Pearce, the housekeeper, has chosen for her after her arrival at Wimpole Street. They are meant to look unalluring, yet Audrey gives such dash to anything she dons that everyone exclaimed on their attractiveness.

Tuesday, 2 July

Audrey, engrossed in singing lessons all morning, had still had no lunch by 3.30. Naturally, she was somewhat tired, though still sweetness and patience personified when she had to submit to a long and rather difficult fitting for her Ascot hat. Leah knew the hat was not ready, but we wanted to see the general effect complete with muff and parasol. In fact, the hat was wrong, and it was by painful degrees, and with many signs of exasperation on the part of Assam, Audrey's Yorkshire terrier, that we bashed into being a hat that is alluring but also hazardous to wear, so that when Eliza is over-excited during the race, the whole construction, with its bows and poppies, will wobble.

Wednesday, 3 July

I had watched Audrey during the tests, wearing almost no make-up and being photographed in a somewhat flat light. One took for granted her charm and vitality, but it was only when the result was magnified hundreds of times, that one realized that, as Jack Warner said, 'She is one in a million'. Somehow, the celluloid accentuates her expressions of tenderness, humour, fun, *hauteur* and plaintive childishness. Her nose and jawline do not conform to the golden rule of Praxiteles yet add enormous character to the photographed result. After seeing herself without eye make-up Audrey pleased me by saying that, in the future, she was going to soft pedal its use. The 'Flemish' look, without any eye make-up, is going to be a surprise. Suddenly, one realizes what a hard look the black liner gives the eye, and how its effect is to close up, and make smaller, the white of the eye. Audrey's appearance without it will be quite a revolution and, let's hope, the end of all those black-eyed zombies of the fashion magazines.

On the Covent Garden set, they were working on the cobble-stones on the uneven ground, but they were not just stamping the shapes from a mould as they usually do in a studio. Each pebble was made with individual care. This makes all the difference between something that is mechanical and something that is vibrant. The effect, if not seen, is definitely sensed on the screen. Gene is to be complimented on attending to these important details. By encouraging the painters to put layer upon layer of different coloured washes he has managed to get them to give the stonework of the church and the arcades a real patina and quality of depth. He is also responsible for the refinement of the brass work: advertising plates, polished signs and gas lamps.

Geoff Allan, a burly, somewhat top-heavy-looking youth from the outskirts of London, has become an expert at 'ageing' clothes. Today he was breaking down Eliza's little jacket in which she first visits Higgins' house. Everyone who had seen the coat in a test agreed that the black velveteen appeared too elegant and rich-looking. In an effort to save the garment, Geoff decided to take drastic measures. He asked me, 'Suppose it doesn't survive?' 'Go ahead. At worst, we'll have to get a new one.' Geoff put the coat in a boiling vat. After a few hours the black velvet had become a cream colour. Geoff now started to make the coat darker, many shades darker. Putting a spoon in dye, he smeared its surface, leaving light patches where the sun might have faded the collars and shoulders. He purposely left paler the material at the edges and in the creases. The coat was then dried out in a furnace. To me, it now looked like something found in an ancient Egyptian tomb: it was as hard and brittle and brown as poppadum. With blazing eyes, Geoff then brought out a wire brush and gave the garment a few deft strokes, saying, 'This bit of pile will soon disappear'. It did. Later Geoff said, with avid enthusiasm, 'I'll take the thing home tonight and sew frogs on it again – coarsely, with black thread, and I'll sew them with my left hand. Then, with my right hand, I'll rip them off. Then I'll knife the seams open here as if it's split. Afterwards, with coarse thread, I'll patch it. Of course, the collar will have to be stained a bit as if Eliza had spilled coffee on it (no, she would drink tea . . . it will have to be tea stains), and there must be greasy marks on the haunches where she wipes her dirty hands. Naturally the skirt will have to be made muddy around the hem, because, you see, she sits when she sells her violets, and the skirt, and petticoats also, would seep up the wet'.

Geoff, like all true artists, is lacking in self-consciousness when talking of his work. He was too busy and in earnest to pay attention to my amusement, as he then brought out Stanley Holloway's dustman clothes. 'This waistcoat must really have a good going-over! It's *much* too new! Oh, and how I do *hate* matching buttons! I'll break this bone one in half. Then I want to make it look as if the sweat had come through Mr Holloway's shirt on to the vest. I'll put his coat, and its double, in acids and then bleach them: it's so much easier if I've got them both at the same time, one in one hand and the other in the other. They're so difficult to match, breaking down and then building up. Can

9 Wilfred Hyde-White as Pickering

10 & 11 Stanley Holloway as
'one of the undeserving poor'

12 Mona Washbourne as Mrs Pearce

13 Eliza seeks vengeance

14 & 15 Audrey wearing extra-girls' clothes

20 Eliza oversteps the bounds of social decorum

21 The Ascot Gavotte

22 The Ascot Parade

23 Gladys Cooper as Mrs Higgins

24 Bina Rothschild as the Queen of Transylvania

you imagine it! I gave Audrey's coat seven different dyeings to make it look as old as that! But I was terribly upset when I found that the crown of her hat fell apart. It became nothing but a handful of black filings.'

Leah, too, was upset when she saw the brim of Eliza's large black hat transformed into something limp and shapeless. 'I'll boil you!' she said, in mock fury. However, she reinforced the brim, gave us a new crown, and the 'feathered thing' looked better than we could have possibly designed it.

This has been music week. Pre-recording by Rex, and tomorrow Audrey does her first solo shut in a cubicle while the orchestra plays outside under André Previn's baton. An ordeal for Audrey, but if her voice is not up to standard she will be the first to admit it. Previn may appear as sleepy as a tapir, but coaxes the best from everyone with his intelligence and patience.

Monday, 15 July

A group of extras, supposedly epitomizing the grand world of opera lovers, appeared dressed in what we considered our most stately clothes. Disaster! All the care, patience and love expended so lavishly seemed to have gone for nothing! Each person was strong enough in his or her own brand of anonymity to kill any costume dead. The glittering capes were for tall women who should have looked like birds of paradise. Here was a dreary gang of runts. They might have been dressed from any old, tarnished rag-bag. What bathos! Something will have to be done about this! From now on, we must take these beautiful garments and allow them to wear the person who is within them. We will have, perhaps, as many as twenty different fittings, each time discarding the wearer until we find a nice suitable body to fit into our finished product.

Another long afternoon spent supervising Audrey's hairdos. Agonizing! I'm not a hairdresser and am inept at using hair, but still I have an instinct for the period and know when proportions are right or wrong. Audrey, too, knows when she looks her best. She says her face is wide and her head flat, and by building the coiffures out at the side this defect becomes exaggerated, so we must play for height. But I contend that unless one sees, at some

point, the shape of the skull, the effect is wooden and clumsy. Although Audrey wishes to be authentic, and is willing to appear plain in the early sequences, she feels that by now, when the 'Rain is in Spain', she should become herself a little more.

The Ballroom coiffure presents the greatest difficulties of all. At an earlier session, I had clumped a wad of curls on to the back of her head and, though the effect was crude, the proportions were right – big, soft and bold. Unfortunately, no record had been taken of this attempt, and Audrey's hairdresser, without documentation, cannot reflect what she has done from one day to another. Today's efforts were disastrous. By some mischance I saw my face reflected in Audrey's triple mirror: it was drawn, and the colour of gorgonzola cheese. Audrey was patient and polite, but behind her expression one could tell that she was tense.

Friday, 19 July

This week has been a swine: never has a Friday evening been more welcome. Audrey, George and I watched the latest tests while Irene, the script girl, wrote down our various criticisms. (These sounded very harsh when later typed out – 'Mr Harrison is much too red or orange – he must stay out of the sun'. 'Try to arrest the turkey-neck with lighting.' 'He needs to wear eye make-up.')

But so many unexpected snags cropped up: the shiny silk braid meant to match the plum colour of Eliza's tuition-dress, came out almost white; and there are often surprises of texture: one of Higgins' nicest suits, of a speckled tweed, gave the effect of the screen twitching. Fairly highly-polished shoes look like patent leather: any brown with red in it comes out crimson and, of course, blue is the devil incarnate.

Eliza's Ascot appearance gave me a nasty jolt. The scarlet poppies on her hat became orange. But who would have guessed that in the long shots the black and white striped lacings and bows would appear green and yellow? I was distressed, and Carol, who made the dress, said that when she heard the news she had to take a couple of aspirins. Audrey, to comfort us, told of how they had to discard a zebra coat, made by Givenchy, in her last film, as that photographed bright yellow.

As for today's attempt at glamour, Audrey's Ball hairdress is like a dowdy bird's nest. George said euphemistically, 'It has no notion'. These tests are always agonizing. Every fault is spotted. No alibis or secrets. No mystery.

Tuesday, 23 July

Twenty extras, whom I had sifted from a hundred others, appeared dressed as Wagnerites. But surely these, too, were a dingy lot. Mercifully, Cukor was a staunch support. 'We must choose again, and go on looking at people until we can find human beings that look as if they are alive!'

Thursday, 25 July

'They're testing the Covent Garden set with the rain machine, and there are some men and women lined up for you on Stage 9.' The women were supposed to be our most stately beauties, the ones who would wear our finest clothes. They were appalling. Buck was rattled when I said they still wouldn't do. It was then decided that we should try to find our paragons from the world of models and mannequins and other such professional beauties.

Monday, 29 July

The week started felicitously with the early morning fitting of Audrey wearing her last dress. It was important that this strike the right mood of romantic individualism. It is of pastille-mauve muslin, and Barbara has made it look as if it has no seams. It is like froth built on Audrey's body.

Joe Hiatt, big and rugged, telephoned to say he had been hanging around just to see Audrey in the dress. He had gazed at it on the stand for fifteen minutes on Friday evening when most people had gone home. He said, 'You know, I'm generally taken by how much a garment costs. This time I'm hypnotized by the dress'.

My visit to the Wardrobe today was a little sad. This is the beginning of the end of a very happy phase. When I had first arrived out here perhaps five inhabitants were to be seen in these vast and beautifully-equipped rooms. Although throughout the shooting of the picture there will be a staff to stay ahead of the necessary costumes, the workers are leaving by the dozens. Morris, the sentimental little tailor whose glorious cloaks are his legacy, will be leaving tomorrow. 'Sad,' said Joe Hiatt, 'but if we kept them all on indefinitely, we'd be broke!' Since early in the year there have been two hundred people, counting the beaders and dyers, working in the Wardrobe. Naturally, all this costs a tidy sum, and maybe the bill for the thousand costumes we have made will run to $500,000.

Tests were shown of the Covent Garden set and the rain effects. When the picture first appeared on the screen, I could not believe this was our 'thing of beauty'. Poor Harry Stradling, our master camera man, was disappointed to see that the scene had been reduced to a Stephens' ink-blue picture postcard: everything sharp, but nothing of atmosphere remained. The longer one looked at the various shots the more one appreciated his difficulties, but Harry was undepressed. He knows what a hard job is in front of him, for this monster camera creates its own banal world unless every effort is made to overcome its commercial, hackneyed point of view. Harry even said he thought it an encouraging start.

Tuesday, 6 August

Action. When I arrived at the studio Joe Hiatt informed me that they want, by Friday next, twenty-four more men and women to be caught in the rain wearing elegant clothes. No panic. The

Wardrobe obeyed with pleasure, and I always enjoy the extravagance of adding colours. Apart from this, a lot of mopping-up operations: servants being fitted for uniforms, liveries and dressing-gowns, Guardsmen, complete with bearskins, and Mrs Pearce's trousseau. (Another felicitous piece of news is that Mona Washbourne is to be our Mrs Pearce. Mona, who hails from Birmingham, has grafted onto her Midlands accent a mellifluous gentility that has heightened the pathos and humour of every role she has played. She was my Mrs Gainsborough in an ill-fated play I once wrote, and created a little work of art for which I shall always love her.)

Meanwhile, Isobel Elsom (our Mrs Eynsford-Hill) was about to be shot on Stage 2. Would I give her the once-over?

A real surprise. While I was away ill with the prevalent virus on Saturday, George Hopkins had spent the day with his staff furnishing Higgins' house with all the stuff we had discovered on our expeditions. He had disposed of the pictures and objects in such an original way that I had no regrets for not having been around. Generally this would have irked me: I like to 'get my fingers on things'. But George could not have done it more brilliantly. Higgins' house is now very much alive and obviously belongs to a strange and original fellow. I don't know if the others on the set (about fifty of them) realized what a remarkable atmosphere we now possess, but certainly no one mentioned it.

Things are really starting to hum, as on Friday the first shots are to be taken involving masses of extras, transport, cabs, props, etc.

In all this turbulence, Wilfred Hyde-White, very calm and casually charming, has just arrived from England and the Goodwood Races to play Colonel Pickering. When asked if he would change into his various clothes for tests, he asked, 'Are they really necessary?'

As always happens in picture-making, during these last few days before shooting starts, most people are panicking a bit, and there are a number of misunderstandings.

I am pessimistic by nature and always anticipate disaster, so it is a particularly trying time for me. Audrey said, 'Everyone's nerves are explosive. Everyone's on edge. It's a difficult time for all of us'. Max Bercutt, Head of Publicity, moaned, 'We thought it was all going to be so pleasant! Everyone's so on edge you'd think we were shooting *Cleopatra*'.

I went to Stage 7 to see the cockney dancers dressed on the set for 'Wouldn't It Be Loverly', Eliza included. At last we had found passable types, and Wardrobe has given them a relationship with figures out of Dickens. I cannot even complain to Hairdressing, and Make-up have carried out my instructions as to types. ('This is a gin drinker, white poultice-face, pink eyes, mauve nose.' 'This is a prissy spinster, neat, birdlike, straggly thin hair, pointed red nose.') Hermes Pan has enlarged the dance in its cinematic scope, and the result is touching. Audrey is a funny, clever dancer. Even her fingertips react in strange ways, and her indomitable smile reflects beleaguered innocence.

Rex was recording for the umpteenth time one of his songs. Never was there a more conscientious actor. Every detail of his work is tackled with as much gravity as a nuclear physicist playing about with a cyclotron. Today, he also set himself the task of learning how to use all the various phonetic apparatuses, supplied to us by Professor Ladefoget of UCLA, as he wished to feel at home handling them in front of the camera. His steely eyes glinted, and his voice was almost breathless with enthusiasm.

Friday, 9 August

Shooting is scheduled to begin next Tuesday, but already Stage 7 is in an uproar: vignettes are to be taken showing the Wagnerians leaving the Opera House and panicking as a squall sends them to cover in the portico of St Paul's Church.

On arrival at the set, my first sight was of a Fuseli-like nightmare. To encourage terrible visions of horses' heads and women's bodies in attitudes of terror, Fuseli would eat large steaks before going to sleep. I had nothing but weak tea in my stomach. Nevertheless, I saw the rain was pouring through the arc lights on to a hackney-carriage drawn by a horse which, as it descended a black, shiny, wet ramp, slipped and fell with the carriage on top of it. Crashes. Shouts. Roars. But no time to bother about Fuseli horses. Anne Laune, with worried eyebrows, was there with a much more urgent question, 'Can we put the magenta on this lady in the jet underslip?'

The rain poured as in the tropics: the waterproof-caped ladies were getting soaked, and my spirits were soaked too. Suddenly I had the panic fear that an age of careful preparations was being cast away in the last-minute haste of battle. So many sorry sights: cloaks that I thought would be the acme of daring elegance being worn by the wrong heads, bodies and legs. To my horror, I spied dropsical women with heads twice the size they should be. But

George Cukor calmed me, saying they would not show in the distance, and in the next shot the crepe hair which was covering their coiffures from the rain would be removed.

But there were other unforeseen disappointments. 'Where is that nice, honey-blonde girl who wore the red foxes?' 'Oh, we lost her.' 'And Miss Smith?' 'She couldn't get her permit.' Good girls lost. Horrors found.

In the middle of the turmoil, my job was to rig out Isobel Elsom in a new costume (for yesterday's tests had made Mrs Eynsford-Hill appear too 'Roman Empressy'), and also to direct the hairdresser, Leonore, in making her appear in the coiffures of her heyday, with the looped bangs à la Alice Long-worth.

Tuesday, 13 August

6 am: Hangman's call. The freeway only slightly populated, but already great life going on at the studio. Coffee canteens popular and, in Make-up, long enfilades of women being painted and coiffed by men and by women – cockneys and grand ladies intermingled.

Outside Stage 7, horse-drawn carriages, as well as antiquated taxis, drays and all manner of market transport, were assembled. There were caravans for wardrobe changes, booths for sound experts, and trailers for stars and important technicians.

I fought the good fight with the hairdressers, and stood over Isobel Elsom to see that she retained the 1913 look. The girls that have finally been chosen for the beauty line-up are tall and dazzling. I was all too glad to be able to admit they looked 'rather spiffing'.

The set was a pewter-coloured Gustave Doré of London come to life, and the proportions are so soaring that the personages appear small in scale – almost like dolls. The flower women and odd market types had real authenticity, and when the rain fell, and the place was flooded, I felt I was back in London. It is a beautiful beginning to any story; the cabs drove through the rain, and the wind machine churned up the puddles and sent sheets of newspaper flying.

Higgins was wearing his old hat. Eliza her boater. Sixty-four photographers from all over the world were there to catch the first shot of the first scene. Now our preparations were at an end. We were in Production.

Wednesday, 21 August

The Heads of various Departments congregate at ten-thirty each morning to see the 'dailies', the rushes of each moving-picture being made in the lot that have just come through from the laboratory. Sometimes the juxtapositions of shots include sequences from stories showing the first Lady President of the United States, the tribulations of an 'out of town' girl in New York, the sex starvations of a group of Marines in the South Pacific, or Bette Davis murdering herself in the guise of her twin sister. Today's *Fair Lady* snippets showed us Eliza in the Inigo Jones' portico. The bird droppings were very authentic, and the flower girl was no simple, sweet little Audrey Hepburn, dressed as a cute cockney with a dab of dirt becomingly placed on her nose: this was a wraughty guttersnipe, full of fight and determination, a real 'rotten cabbage leaf'. This should make the metamorphosis from scruffy sparrow to bird-of-paradise even more dramatic.

I wanted to congratulate Audrey on her appearance, so went down on to the set for a word with her. I watched her being shot, listening to Higgins telling Pickering that, but for her appalling accent, Liza could be passed off as a duchess. The play of expression on her face was such that one could almost see her brain at work with ideas that followed one another like a succession of pictures.

Today the market looked very real with characters lying about on old potato sacks; it even smelt authentic with the vegetables getting a bit high. My fears about these scenes being less effective if shot here than in London had not been well-founded. By distorting the proportions of the buildings the whole panorama had an eerie and foreboding poignancy.

A sort of 'after storm' calm prevails; the technical crew go about their business with the least amount of fuss, the hairdressers and make-up assistants have brought out their knitting, the extras their novelettes or science fiction, and the electricians the trade newspapers.

Thursday, 22 August

At lunch-time Audrey, wearing her dirty hair and face, came into my room to say 'Ullow'. Every dawn Audrey has to have her hair covered with grease, then with a lot of brown Fuller's Earth. The effect is really dirty, and psychologically must be very depressing. Tiring, too: it takes another hour to wash out the dirt before going home after the day's shooting. Audrey said she was beginning to warm up in her part, but was sad that on the first

73

day's shooting she didn't get into the right groove; had been too strident, her eyes bugged, and she hadn't felt deeply enough. 'Unless you know a character so well that you can relax completely, it somehow doesn't work. I see what it should be now that it's too late,' she laughed, wistfully.*

For certain people involved, motion-picture making, while in production, must be a long sustained strain. The star, through no fault of his own, must sometimes repeat a scene for a seemingly ludicrous number of times. It is then that technique becomes a dominant factor. Audrey is remarkably disciplined: her memory never at fault, she appears on the set word perfect, and she can give exactly the same performance over and over again. She confessed, however, that yesterday's pea-shelling scene had been the greatest strain for she had to eat so many raw peas; at best, she does not care for them even when they are at their youngest and smallest, but having had to eat a bushel, of huge Californian peas out of their inflated pods, she then went home to dinner and was served duck and green peas!

Tuesday, 27 August

On the set Audrey was still doing 'Loverly'. Finding it difficult to work to different 'play-backs' she had been nervously taut most of the day. Now, by mid-afternoon, she was tired out. Her hairdresser was massaging the back of her neck: everyone sorry for her, and the atmosphere tense. I got an 'OK' from the Director for the coat Liza must wear in the next sequence (the one Geoff had worked on), and the bell having sounded for silence, I crept out of the building. I was canny, for Audrey later became too pent-up to allow either of the two 'still' photographers assigned to this picture to remain on the set. She explained to them that the one eye of the movie camera does not disturb her, but their smaller ubiquitous lenses were distracting. Bob Willoughby and Mel Traxel have the responsibility of recording photographically every scene taken by the moving camera, as well as showing the progress of the production. It is a long and soul-destroying assignment at the best of times. Mel later whimpered that conditions were much less favourable than on any other picture he has ever worked: they are not allowed to photograph during rehearsals, and for most of the time must try to hide themselves

* It was not too late. This first scene was later re-shot.

74

in dark corners. 'I wear this black suit just not to be seen: of course, if I were invisible, it would make my job easier, but it's been an up-hill struggle just to get the most ordinary shots – let alone anything interesting!' If conditions are hard for these two, acceptable photographers imagine the courage it takes to brazen out my presence when I appear before George and Buck Hall wearing flamboyantly light-coloured clothes and a planter's straw hat, with my Rolleiflex in my hand and my pockets bulging with film.

Thursday, 29 August

Anxiety started with a message early that Mr Cukor had seen the tests of Gladys Cooper and Isobel Elsom and wanted me on set immediately after I had seen them. I feared the worst. There were several things about the rushes I did not like: Isobel Elsom's dress makes her appear too big, must be changed, but George had spotted many other faults. Mona Washbourne's bosom too triangular, and her clothes look too new: maids too high-busted, wigs too wiggy, and a real calamity about Gladys Cooper – everyone, including Steve Trilling, who sent me a note to say so, was shocked by her test: the dress and hairdo blamed.

By now my battle with the hairdressers is at its peak. After ordering the wrong-shaped wig for Gladys Cooper they now inform me there is no authority to order a new wig. What really gripes me is having to scrap her evening dress. Of all we have made I feel that this was the most original. At the news of its demise even stalwart Anne Laune collapsed.

Nothing really pleasant happened at any time of the day: photographing on the sound stage I was made to feel *de trop*: I had to stay late as tomorrow we start the long siege in Higgins' house. Mona Washbourne, as Mrs Pearce, works tomorrow for the first time but, although we had entirely altered her bodices, at the moment she has nothing to wear. In order to 'age' her dress Geoff drowned it in a bucket of 'soup'. Being made of a genuinely old material it came out in shreds. Another will have to be made by seven o'clock tomorrow morning.

Tuesday, 3 September

'What exactly are you doing in Hollywood?' 'Fighting hair-

75

dressers.' Is this really what I want to be doing at my time of life?

Alan Lerner has just returned from Capri. Of course this was the holiday season and Capri still existed. When I asked him if he would be staying here long, he admitted no, he was leaving at the end of the week for – guess where? – Istanbul. Alan has the grand style in everything: he thinks nothing of suggesting retakes of certain scenes which would entail several days of extra work.

Wednesday, 4 September

I wrote to my sister Nancy, wishing her many happy returns, only to discover that I was one month in advance of the correct date. This shows in what a strange state of timelessness one lives in Hollywood.

I felt I ought, before leaving this evening, to take some pictures of Eliza's first arrival at Higgins' room, and her asking the Professor to give her lessons.

The actors were all pretty whacked with long rehearsals. The heat of the lights kept the 'demolition squad' of make-up artists and hairdressers busy with their last-minute moppings and renovations with powder and comb.

Audrey, rather pooped, posed for some pictures out in the hall, away from the concourse, but she knew she looked tired. The Director seemed a bit on edge, and his attention focused on the crew. 'Quiet! We will have quiet: no more talking for the rest of the picture: everyone stay out of sight!' Steve Trilling was on the set; his cheerfulness is commendable. I felt ashamed when he said, 'You are happy about everything, aren't you?' and I had grudgingly, but not enthusiastically, to admit 'Yes.'

Thursday, 5 September

I am apt to criticize as extravagant waste some of the techniques of the studio: the amount of paper work and written instructions that are sent to all and sundry, the amount of 'help' required by the Unions, the hanging around on the part of the technicians. Before production started the property men would sit about for days on end doing nothing. But as soon as the cameras start grinding, and their jobs have started, they are kept on the hop. There is no denying that Warner's, who have been making films for forty years, have evolved a technique that can cope with most eventualities. Poor old George Hopkins has had a hard time since Covent Garden market was in use, each day having to supply flowers, vegetables, fruit and a million unexpected things. If instructions weren't committed to paper, chaos could break out.

Messages on all sides to say that Cukor wanted to see my designs for the new Gladys Cooper costumes. Fortunately, I had one or two ideas at the back of my mind, and a few quick moments in which to slam out some colour sketches, so that I was able to take these onto the set. While I waited for a convenient moment of the Director's time, I watched a long scene being taken over and over again. Sometimes an aeroplane would be heard approaching, and all had to wait, or the sound man would have some less obvious difficulty. Meanwhile, the Director gave his instructions:—

'Be quick on – "But what is that for?" (pointing at a handkerchief). Don't stand before he tells you to! Don't get so low in the chair! Don't cover your face with your hands!'

Once or twice Rex dried up. Once, instead of asking Eliza: 'How much do you propose to pay me for the lessons?' he used the word 'letters'. Eliza had to continue . . . 'A lady-friend of mine gets French lessons for eighteenpence an hour from a real French gentleman . . .' Confusion and laughter broke out. Rex added, 'That would be a different sort of play!' Mona Washbourne, Wilfred Hyde-White and Rex Harrison were highly amused, but Audrey, like Queen Victoria, was not.

When they broke for the camera to be re-loaded Rex was so concentrated in the part of Higgins that he was oblivious to anything else: he did not see me as I stood close by, his eyes unable to focus on ordinary everyday things. Wilfred Hyde-White is always casually disarming and charming. When I asked how he was getting on, he shrugged: 'Oh, you know how it is; it's always the same thing with these films.' I complimented him on his rushes. He joked, 'Oh, I am always good in rushes, but never any good in the finished picture.'

The Director, like some deep-sea fish, loomed in one direction then switched to a tangent, always with lower jaw working alarmingly. Once a 'take' was in the can, his head lopped to the side. I showed him the new Cooper drawings; he liked them in a flash, then talked about the cape of her Ascot dress not having the *brio* of my sketch – 'And the hat is not so well put on her head'. His eye is extraordinarily quick, for although he had seen my original sketch for only a second, and the test for a moment too, yet he remembered every detail. Discussing Gladys' coiffure, he suggested, with fingers contorted tortuously, something soft and romantic in the Greek style. But how to achieve this? Few of the hairdressers that I have come across have a lightness of hand, and when they have pickaxed the hair into a wooden mass, they enclose it in a firm net so that it cannot possibly have any life. When I telephoned to Gladys to consult with her and ask if she had any suggestions as to how her hair could be worn with additions, she sidetracked the issue and said, 'No good hairdresser has ever been a woman. I cannot imagine how the tradition started that film studios have men to do the make-up and women the hair. There are only good men hairdressers. Sidney Guillaroff is the kingpin here: no one else exists.'

It seems that the campaign I am waging is nothing new in the history of motion pictures. In fact, the difficulties are traditional under the system whereby the technicians are responsible to the Head of the Department. Many of the hairdressers are terrified lest I (a mere outsider) ask them to create an effect which can be criticized in the projection room as slipshod work, and therefore reflects against the Department.

The same applies to 'sound'. The engineer will not record a whisper for fear that someone in the projection room will say, 'Can't hear! What's he saying? He's not speaking loud enough!' The 'culprit' on the boom is not there to defend himself.

Likewise the Camera Department says, 'We don't do it that way,' or the man from the Music Department is also likely to say, 'What am I going to say to the Head of the Department when he sees the rushes?' To depart from the accepted formula of excellence takes the bloom off some reputations. This is one of the vestiges of the days when Hollywood studios were factories churning out hundreds of slick pictures each year with which to feed the ever-ravenous public. The result is to bring so much down to the level of the 'norm', and to keep freshness, or even reality, at bay.

Wimpole Street has been erected. From the ground plans I hadn't

realized it would fill an entire sound stage, for it is to be used for only minor sequences of the picture. Another surprise was to find on what a vast scale the tents of Ascot were being laid out. The trellis-work has arrived, and there is enough wood here to make a whole city. The effect of the serried arches will be like lace, or like a series of doilies. It should give all sorts of opportunities to the cameraman for variations of light.

In the Art Department the models of the Ballroom unit were now ready, the double curved staircase, the long anteroom or corridor and the Ballroom itself. I was pleased that these sets would not only be pretty, but as unusual as we dare be in a picture in this somewhat naturalistic vein.

The pieces of this vast tapestry we are working upon are slowly being woven together: the Assistant Director's cross plot is ticked off day by day. Today, according to the chart:

> 'Higgins explains terms to Eliza. After Pickering remonstrates, Eliza accepts.'

Other days' work in front of us, according to Buck Hall's legend are:

> 'Mrs Pearce succeeds in disrobing Eliza.'
> 'Higgins uses marbles in teaching, leading to "Rain in Spain".'
> 'Higgins gives tart to bird, infuriating Eliza.'
> 'Eliza meets Society. Freddie gives her his bet.'
> 'Higgins astonished, tells Mother Eliza's gone.'
> 'Doolittle and pals run out of pub.'
> 'Higgins meets Mother amid general confusion.'

The dreaded heat-wave is upon us, and the temperature in the Wardrobe is such that the flowers the women bring in from their gardens to put in jam pots on their work-tables sag over the sides, and the women themselves sag. Yet still their enthusiasm continues unabated. Leah and I worked on the last twenty-five hats for Ascot, and had much fun in doing so, inventing shapes that made everyone around roar with laughter.

Tuesday, 10 September

Nothing wrong with today, the activity was of my own doing: Mort Lichter, of Publicity, with the face of a charmingly sad parrot, had arranged for me a big photographic bout in the still studio, with three models in relays of clothes and hats. Involved are hairdressers, special wardrobe assistants, and a huge crew, including one man to stand about to manage the wind machine which we might use in a few of the shots. The sitting was made harder for me because the electricians have their way of doing things, and these are not mine, so that I had to fight every inch of the way to prevent their putting on 'fill-in' lights without telling me, and obliterating shadows whenever possible. It was difficult to get an effect of soft light that possessed enough candle power needed for colour film. The lights were hot and my feet stuck to the concrete floor. But I was pleased with the work.

80

'Audrey is arriving momentarily.'

Miss Hepburn's special make-up man arrives, then her own hairdresser and two publicity men. Finally the star shuffles in. Very tired and pale, in a shirt with her Cockney hat as Eliza. It is a paradox, the guttersnipe being treated like Royalty. Audrey is given this treatment because every moment of her expensive time is taken up with some activity that has to do with her portrayal as Eliza. There is seldom a 'let up' for her with every moment taken with fittings, tests or journalistic interviews. She appears on each day's shooting schedule, but today she was through her scenes early so was able to give me twenty precious, long-awaited minutes to pose in the studio.

In the old days a movie actress was able to create a fake image. By being photographed only at certain angles in a certain light, the star managed to establish herself as a figment of her own imagination. Often the hoax continued successfully and profitably for many a year. But nowadays the screen has become more earthy, photography more candid, and the direction more intimate. Unless the actress is a real human being her limitations will be obvious to the far more sensitive audiences of today. In this sitting Audrey, whose personal character makes her, with these new requirements, the star she is today, also proved to be an ideal subject for still photography.

The 'dailies' or 'rushes' can be extremely monotonous. Every line of every scene is repeated from various angles many times over. If four people are in the shot, the rushes can become a severe test of endurance. Granted that the cutter prefers a wide choice and that the Director likes to cover himself, I still would have thought that there were only one or two angles that were psychologically correct for each scene.

Chose colours for jockeys' uniforms and for the repainting of those antiquated automobiles which can be coralled from those idle, but clever, men who sit back while hiring out for exorbitant sums an old-crock Daimler or a discarded taxicab.

A messy, uncreative day, full of incident, but nothing adding up to anything. A friendly visit from nice Rachel Harrison, with her dulcet Welsh accent and an ugly hound-dog, was a whiff of friendliness that I felt very much in need of. I realize that every relationship on the lot has to do with work. After a bit this becomes part of the prison sentence. Not that I want to sit around indulging in desultory conversation: I take conversation too seriously to feel that it should be gratuitous. It is fine to go out for a drink and a talk, or dinner and talk, but cursory talk round corners of the lot is debilitating. When one has so much on one's mind, even exchanges of bonhomie, *en passant*, are an unnecessary effort.

Friday, 13 September

Jack Warner rang with a whole heap of praises for the work I had done while he was on a business trip in Europe. Most important of all, he said that I was probably as depleted as he was: he was off to Palm Springs for a long weekend, so why didn't I take a few days off? 'It's no good operating when you're tired; besides, you're your own boss, you don't have to punch a clock – do as you feel.' In fact, I have felt I was punching a clock, and have been pricked by guilt every time the police cop at the gates has marked down an early departure or late arrival. However, I am told these marks are more in the nature of a census, so that if another fire breaks out, they will know who is or is not missing.

Joe Hiatt came in. 'May some of the men in the background wear black frock-coats?' 'Yes.' 'That "yes" has saved us a lot of money, and may they have black hats?' 'No, grey.' 'Then we'll cable to Moss Bros. in London again.'

Joe continued, 'Will it be all right if some of the men at the Ball wear patent leather lace shoes and not pumps?' 'Yes.' 'That "yes" has made me 850 bucks.' Joe then informed me, 'We're going through the logistics of the Ascot scene. Nothing is resolved so far, but we have our problems. One of 'em is space. Now the women's hats, being so enormous, will take up four times the usual room allotted for the hairdressers to put on wigs and hats. Imagine, we have to put out one hundred and fifty hats in a row, and we have to organise a special team to look after them. Then we have to decide what happens to the ladies in the lunch break. I think it will be better if we give 'em a thirty minute interval, and feed 'em with a box-lunch. We will have to arrange space in the section where they come and get into their dresses. There's the

82

problem of how, when they're dressed, we get them "On Stage".
In the script the horses rush by in front of them: the only place
you can get the horses to run at speed is the usual entrance for the
actors, and we can't have the women coming in on the special
dirt track they're laying for the horses. Another thing we have to
realize – for days on end we'll have these women on our hands
from 6 am. – 6 pm. And I don't want 'em to go to the Ladies
Room. I don't even want 'em to sit down!' Of course, we'll have
to have special big leaning rest-boards built, and this is a question
of thousands of dollars, but we can't have the guild on our hands.

Monday, 15 September

I was in no hurry to wake up as, *grace à* Mr Warner, I was taking
a day off. Without the usual stampede to get to the lot on time,
the realization of my accumulated exhaustion caused a limpness
in every limb. I yawned without stop. Dragging myself to the
hotel swimming pool I took a belly-flop. Intending to browse
through a long-discarded novel, I nodded and dozed. Only the
arrival of Jack and Jim brought me back to consciousness. They
were to take me to lunch at that Californian equivalent of an
oriental bazaar – the Farmers' Market. Here the milling crowds
gape at birds and beasts in pet shops, devour dishes of all nation-
alities or imbibe strawberry juice and coconut milk: here one
has the impression that every day is a holiday; everyone in good
humour – as well they should be. For the polished mounds of
fruit and vegetables are as large as only California can produce.
But not merely local delicacies are displayed: exotic hampers,
made up of Mexican and oriental fruit, are 'gift wrapped' with
such brilliance that it would seem a sacrilege to destroy the
symmetry by helping oneself to a lichee or a custard apple.

Jack, Jim and I, replete with exotic dishes and outrageous
'freezes', and laden with loot; baskets, lanterns, and writing paper
adorned with the heads of pug-dogs, continued our sightseeing
down-town. The Bradbury Building is the Los Angelean equivalent of heavy Victoriana. In a vast inner patio black iron-work and
cedar-wood panelling create an effect of great solidity with black
cage-like elevators going up and down in a leisurely and serene
manner between the tall balconied floors. This relic of a past era
still pronounces its essence with extraordinary authority and has
quite splendidly fought successfully the demolition squads.

So, too have the Watts Towers. These were built, over a period of thirty-three years, entirely alone by Rodia, an Italian, who came to this country at the age of twelve and worked as a tile-setter on the nearby railway line. Made of steel frames covered with mesh and mortar, these towers soar to a height of a hundred feet and, at first sight, they might be miniature oil derricks or part of a Gothic cathedral. They are linked together with cement arches, pavilions and labyrinths into which Rodia has pressed a mosaic of broken plates, Seven-Up bottles and any highly coloured rubbish he could find. Rodia, with no drawing board designs, scaffolding or machine equipment, and using only the simple tools of a tile-setter and a window-washer's belt, built these strange pinnacles and arbours in the face of ridicule and hostility. The result is of a magical fantasy reminiscent only of Gaudi's cathedral in Barcelona, the burial pinnacles of Bangkok, or the facteur Cheval's house at Hauterives.

At the age of seventy-three, his work completed, Rodia, disappointed at man's ingratitude, left this forlorn and impoverished neighbourhood, apparently to forget his thirty-three years' work. At any rate, he is reluctant to talk about it, and says, 'If your mother dies, and you have loved her very much, maybe you don't speak of her.' Today, Rodia lives as an unknown retired railwayman in Norfolk, California, but his towers, glistening in the sunlight, are the most interesting work of art to be found in all Los Angeles.

In 1957 the Building Department issued an order for their removal. A committee was hurriedly formed to preserve them as works of art. A test was made to prove whether or not the towers were a public danger. Rodia's home-made architecture stood all strain and stress. The towers were saved, and tended carefully for the delight of those who come from all the world over to contemplate this supreme facet of artistic expression.

On our way home through the undistinguished, and almost indistinguishable, boulevards, Jack and Jim showed me the best in modern architecture: the Perpetual Building, built by Edward Stone, of poured white concrete. With its slightly Arabian honeycomb façade, it succeeds in bringing imagination and originality to a thriving commercial building. Its daring use of bad taste is entirely acceptable because of the refinement with which it is executed. The same, unfortunately, cannot be said about the strangely swirling, cantilevered building on Rodeo

Drive which Frank Lloyd Wright planned but which, like the Guggenheim Museum in New York, was executed by others in materials different from those he intended. In fact, they both appear to be made of compressed nougat without the cherries.

A married couple returns to the hotel suite next door to my room. The walls are paper-thin, and I hear the husband crying in delighted wonderment, 'More flowers! And roses! These cost $20.00 a dozen!'

Tuesday, 17 September

My Wardrobe friends are my best friends here: no matter to what trial or tribulation I put them they regard me with tolerance and sympathy.

Today Isobel Elsom was being hung with tent-like folds that were nearer to camouflage than dress design.

Rex Harrison was suddenly beset with the immediate problem of what he should wear during the various 'Lesson' scenes. Naturally a chart was made out for this even before we ordered his various garments. But Rex likes facing himself with such problems at only the very last moment. Sometimes I can sway him, but often, on closer consideration, he decides to put on a completely different outfit. Yet he needs my presence in order to take a firm line from which he can argue the pros and cons. It is typical of his meticulousness that he spends an hour trying on three different ties.

The English group out here frat with one another in almost inexhaustible *camaraderie*. Wilfred Hyde-White, nodding with pursed lips and head well down, carries the airmail edition of the *Daily Telegraph* folded under his arm, Mona Washbourne throws back her head and emits a guffaw while Gladys Cooper, with unquenchable vitality, gives a galvanized report on the opening of London's National Theatre. Stanley Holloway has a tireless sense of humour: anything that strikes him as deeply comic remains with him for always. His old jokes come to life again with extraordinary freshness; he remembers early lyrics, and laughs as heartily when recalling the gags of George Robey, or the days of concert parties and 'The Co-Optimists', as when he first heard them. Stanley is a very lovable person. In his unassuming way he is a great gentleman. Today Mrs Stanley

85

Holloway was high-piping her congratulations on the morning's news that the Queen is expecting a fourth child.

'It's raining!' gasped a girl in Wardrobe. The word soon went round. Everybody is excited for rain is an event. The natives are clad from head to toe in plastic, the English love the downpour and feel at home. For two days we enjoyed the grey cool after the blistering heat.

Joe Hiatt rings: 'This is your morale booster speaking.' Joe is always the one who brings good tidings. Gordon Bau, Head of Make-up, had rung to say he had never seen such costumes as those of Ascot, and were the Ball dresses as good? He was trying to invent, for the ladies, a new body 'make-up' so that they would not smear the dresses during the days of shooting. This was a real compliment.

On the set George and Gene were running through the routine for the next scene, a complicated manoeuvre in which Doolittle is leaving the Higgins' house and bumps into the 'washed-up nicely' Eliza. Gene, very absorbed and serious, reiterated, 'You pan to her ass. Doolittle smacks it.'

The books in the top of the library are too brightly coloured. Audrey has too prettified hair with unsuitable *chic* side curls, and Mona Washbourne's wig has completely lost its style. By now the hairdressers are really doing what they like. A halt must be called. I wonder if it is my own fault that it all falls so far short of fun?

Went to see Hermes Pan's Ascot gavotte, and showed him drawings by Sem and Drian to illustrate the Forzane* slouche. Later, he and I chose dancing girls. It seems that Hermes has trouble with the Guild in getting people who are not on their books and, naturally, those we like the best are not. Hermes keeps a wonderful calm, perhaps imposed by his strong religious beliefs.

Today 'close-ups' were being re-taken of 'Wouldn't It Be

* The last of the pre-1914 war cocottes, who walked with her hips thrust forward and one foot always trailing.

Loverly' and 'Why Can't The English?' This puts the schedule behind one day. Here again, as if life had stood still, there turned up the same old recalcitrant extras. Their re-appearance brought back to mind the hectic tension of the first week's shooting. Luckily, that sort of frenzy has to die down eventually.

Rex sang his song over and over again with such perfection that one could not but be amazed at his technique. The range of sound that he produces is extraordinarily varied: there are deep notes that have survived since his first days of stage training, and he is not afraid of becoming almost falsetto. He knew he was performing well and was highly keyed. He was unaware that he was surrounded by people, yet submitted like a prince to the titivations of the make-up and hairdressers. After every take his sweating brow was mopped, then the mirror placed in front of him while absorbedly he replaced his hat.

At one moment we were all alarmed to see sparks and flashes of light issuing from the outer periphery of the set; an electrical fuse box had caught fire. Thirty workmen ran in the direction of the blaze, smoke went up to the skies. I envisaged the incendiary of the whole of Covent Garden, and a stampede to the doors. But Rex went on looking into the glass, patting his tie, and with great gravity asking, 'Is the camera reloaded?' Fortunately, the fire was put out before the cyclorama went up in flames – for this would have been serious – and Rex continued to sing without a 'dry'. During these long takes Cukor swayed backwards and for-wards with a wide, beatific grin on his face, and indeed anyone with appreciation for artistry of a very high order cannot but have been impressed by Rex's virtuosity. His phrasing is masterly: with the emphasis and 'throw away' lines so perfectly balanced, the line is firm and as delicately trod as an expert tight-rope acrobat. This surely was Rex at the very peak of his career.

The fire alarm was soon forgotten but the climate on the set itself continued to be quite inflammable and, since I deemed it unwise to start any photography today, I beat it.

I knew, when taking on this assignment, that it would mean exiling myself from the rural countryside of Wiltshire for at least the whole of one Spring, Summer, and Autumn. But this large scale venture was one worth making great sacrifices for. I would have been extremely upset if any other designer had pocketed this particular plum. And I am being paid well.

Why, then, is it that I am in a mood where I know I must 'slog on' long past the point of enchantment? The work never fails to be interesting; the talent, kindness, and willingness of my assistants never fails to astound. Nothing but enthusiasm and gratitude emanates from Jack Warner and his office. How have I failed my Director? He does not complain of the quality of my work, or that it is behind schedule. Yet if I had perpetrated something so ugly that it jeopardized the work of all connected with the picture, and each piece of furniture or length of wall-paper I had chosen was an offence, my presence on the set could not create an atmosphere more fraught with tenseness. This is a disappointing state of affairs. A gut-grinding pain seldom leaves me, even when spending the evenings with friends who sense

my preoccupation yet are loth to mention it; their secret com-
miseration for something they know nothing of only causes me
further distress which haunts me during the night.

To brave the opposition on the set becomes more and more of
an effort the longer I delay putting in appearances.

Friday, 20 September

The very private and personal ritual of preparing for each day's
sortie starts for me in my hotel-cell at an early hour with the
pulling of the cord to part the curtains above the door. Through
the fanlight I see either a hard, blue sky, or else a mist through
which the sun will probably break after my departure for the
studio. Opening the mosquito-meshed door, I receive the folded
copy of the *New York Times* Western Edition, its headlines blazing
with bomb outrages against the negroes in Alabama, or President
Kennedy cutting, or not cutting, taxes, giving, or not giving, aid
to Vietnam or to Europe. I notice that the patio-garden is 'in
between times', and that there are bare patches of earth in the beds
where clumps of hollyhocks and marguerites have had their brief,
sun-scorched day

Now starts my ridiculous weight-saving and expense-saving
routine of boiling some water for my weak-tea and melba-toast
breakfast. If I have been able to save some butter from a former
'room service' dinner in my room, it is preciously produced from
the frigidaire. The frugal breakfast over, a stampede follows to
write this diary, to shave electrically, and to plunge into the pool.
While drying myself with one hand, with the other I ring the
front desk, 'Any letters?' 'Yes, you've hit the jackpot today.' Of
course, by the time I have greedily devoured the news from home,
blown down a roll of magazines, hoping that one day they will
uncurl themselves, and am in the car on the freeway, the radio
programme of Mannings' Piano Parade has given place to the
benefits of a posturepoedic mattress. 'Sleeping on a Seeley is like
sleeping on a cloud,' they tell me. While I am thinking of various
Seeleys I know – there was a Nigel Seeley at Harrow, a Victor
Seeley at Cambridge, and a Vera Seeley from Nottingham – and
wondering which one would best to sleep on, the advertising has
switched and I am enjoined: 'Picture a king-sized, juicy steak, a
savoury "sarce" at its side, a "tarst" green salad. And to drink?
Why, of course . . .' 'A cocktail in the Paris studio of a couturier

designer? A sightseeing tour of the city? A fabulous table at the famous Lido? The Cancan? You can be a real Parisian. *C'est magnifique*, what a week, if you fly TWA!'

A news bulletin intersperses its various items with a musical chord, 'Ping! The President returns to Washington. Pang! Three bodies found in a landslide. Pong!'

The cop at the auto-gate greets me in an off-hand way. Perhaps he has heard complaints about me? Or perhaps he's disgusted at my late arrival? Too bad! In any case, let's brazen it out.

Chekhov again: Apropos the artist – 'he is a responsible person under contract to his conscience . . . he is in duty bound to battle with his fastidiousness and soil his imagination with the grime of life'.

Monday, 23 September

My aeroplane returned from San Francisco at eight o'clock so, perhaps in order to prove that I *could* arrive on the lot, I went this morning to show myself on the set. Mrs Pearce and two maids were about to give Eliza a bath, and when the ragamuffin protested, her clothes were snatched off. The bathroom looked very authentic, but the imitation steam got in Eliza's eyes and she frowned throughout the day.

A great disappointment! Owing to a question of money, Fritzi Massary is not going to play the part of the Queen of Transylvania. She had originally said she would be very expensive, but it seems her agent has opened his mouth so wide that 'Casting' is thunderstruck. I was so appalled that in desperation I rang Fritzi to know if she wouldn't change her mind.

'But it would be such fun!' I shouted.

'No, no, my dear boy, I am beyond the years of fun. If I do a week's work they must pay me well. It's thirty years since I retired. What's the use upsetting myself for nothing? I'm not disappointed,' she said.

'But I am! Bitterly so!' Who will we find who has Fritzi's *panache*?

The picture grinds on. No one can be hysterical all the time, so necessarily there are periods of calm. But how long this will last nobody knows. Maybe a microphone shadow will spoil a perfect take. Perhaps the lesser technicians, electricians, prop-men, hair-dressers, dressers, and all those others of unknown categories sitting around are to blame.

The demand for sitting-space is acute. Only important people like actors and Director have chairs allotted. If a comfortable perch is spotted, it is a case of 'finding's keeping', and there is no nonsense about 'ladies first'. The long planks of wood or steel laid on trollies are extremely inviting, but they are dangerous perches and are apt to collapse with an appalling noise which may cause the ruin of a 'take' – than which nothing worse in the world of picture-making exists. It is often necessary to seek information from some person whose very job may necessitate his being all day on the set. Even though your whispering cannot be picked up by the microphone, the Assistant Director's ears are hyper-sensitive instruments. Certainly 'shop talk' is the most fascinating of all, and the technicians discuss their problems until, suddenly, a sound as of steam beginning to escape from a funnel is the Direc-tor's personal plea for silence. For some time one can hear a pin drop. But the ebullient sea of whispering starts again. Each man is really only interested in his own job, and doesn't concern himself with anyone else's. He doesn't give a damn about that man in a toupet over there holding forth into the mike. Perhaps some of us occasionally wonder if the other man's job is not the easier. ('He' arrives late; 'she' gets away early; 'they' have a day off), and sometimes we feel that perhaps the stars are the only ones who get the best of this peculiar world. Yet the stars' ascendancy is often of short duration, while the prop-men and electricians go on being employed in the same studio until they retire at a natural old age.

The whispering starts again, this time the reaction is more serious. Like steer, the 'lower personnel' are driven to the outer periphery of the studio. Recently a huge black curtain has been erected behind which the recalcitrants cower so that their presence will not be a distraction to sensitive artists.

Tuesday, 24 September

Poor old George Hopkins, suffering from high blood pressure and almost total exhaustion, had to call the doctor in the middle of the night. His nose bled like a torrent until he was given the biggest injection since the flood. Today he mumbled sadly about the difficulties with the Unions. It seems the people who are making the draperies for the tents for Ascot think they should be laying the green-sward. The green-sward setters think they should be doing the awnings for the tents. Everyone is fighting someone.

Meanwhile, negotiations are still under way to procure tall and beautiful young ladies for the big race sequences. The Guild says they can supply the types we need but, so far, no good. Last night a great concourse – everybody they had. The verdict: a rotten lot! Where are the show-girls of Hollywood? It seems they have fewer opportunities here since large film musicals have gone out of fashion, so they have returned to Broadway. Meanwhile, the Union forbids us to use just anyone who strikes our fancy.

The semi-parasitical way of life of the extras, the general anxious softness of their lives, the sycophancy towards powerful 'king extras', and a dependency on the Assistant Director's favours – all these things create a brittle anonymity. To avoid the possibility of their being identified as individuals who could be spotted in an early shot – and thus make themselves ineligible for the crowd-scene that will take place in a different context – they have developed a protective colouring; they present a sea of faces that are colourless, lifeless, and hapless. When their sub-terfuges of sleeping behind back-drops, or hiding, are discovered, and they are shepherded on to the set, they melt into one another like innocuous masks of unrecognizability. Occasionally glaring with sullen pride at their wrist-watches to show their displeasure, or sadly whispering their daytime grievances, they acquire the spirit of the 'lumpen', the despondent, but unsocial mass.

Wednesday, 25 September

The sun was burning, even when I had my early swim in the pool. By the time I drove through the auto-gate at the studio, the temperature was higher than any day of the year. By the afternoon it had reached 107°.

For most of the day I was firmly incarcerated in my air-con-ditioned room, painting some costume designs with one hand and answering the telephone with the other. But visiting the set in the late afternoon I watched a Kiplingesque scene. Eliza singing 'Just You Wait, 'Enery 'Iggins', orders the troops to raise their guns and fire and, as an addition to the stage version of the play, we now see the King and the soldiers materialize for the execution.

A troop of extras, rigged out by Geoff, in scarlet uniforms, bear-skins and muskets, were sweating into their large, false mous-taches. The King was cloaked in velvet and miniver. Eliza, gesticulating frantically, wore a tiered dress of thick wool. The ice machine had to be switched off for each 'take' as it made a whirring sound. The heat on the set can be imagined.

Thursday, 26 September

A flood of female persons poured into my rooms to be dressed for Ascot and the Ball. Some of the girls I had originally discarded,

had, nevertheless, again stormed the compound, and it was tricky to get rid of them. One's instincts in spotting a delinquent are generally sound and, of course, these were the ones who proved the most difficult and unco-operative. This is a hectic business, made more difficult by conflicting opinions and personal idio-syncrasies. If we had not been so harassed everyone connected with Wardrobe would have realized that this was the great moment when all the dresses made on the stands were, at last, coming to life. But the flurry put all ideas out of our heads, and one acted merely upon the reflexes of instinct. Many dresses that had been completed five months ago came out from the closets as complete surprises, and the human element gave a quite different dimension to certain garments that we have only seen on stands.

The heat was a record – 110° in Burbank. When pretty, dimpled, Moyna McGill came to be rigged out as Lady Boxington the sweat ran down from her forehead and dropped off her button nose like a water-spout.

In between emergency calls to the set, or to the Art Department, I tried to get on with some designs. I took a sort of fanatic's delight in thrashing myself to further efforts, and ran backwards and forwards between the various Departments and my office like a soul in torment.

Monday, 30 September

Joe Hiatt said euphemistically 'This week's going to be tough for you. We have to dress four hundred people in ten days, and we will send 'em into you in relays of ten'. Joe, more than anyone else, realizes the efforts that goes into the various aspects of this work and a more sympathetic and understanding Head of Wardrobe could not be imagined.

A posse of young women were already entrenched in my rooms on my arrival, and once again the game was played of fitting human bodies into the outer shells that had already been made. The hat belonging to one costume would not look its best on a certain woman so the whole outfit must be changed. A grey-haired dowager mustn't wear a chinchilla hat as the camera will confuse where hat and hair begin, so another switch. Among those who appeared was one glorious young English girl from Sandy in Bedfordshire. She makes Elizabeth Taylor a suet pudding in comparison, but, unlike most Americans, who seem to have given up the habit, this stupid girl spoilt the effect of her calm, Canova marble serenity, by chewing gum.

There are ever continuing surprising aspects of this job: little did I realize that I would be earning my living by playing a sort of game of heads, bodies and legs with human beings. Yet this is just what this phase of the operation consists of: many discoveries are made. One imagines that a certain girl will be good in a particular style of costume only to discover that she must dress in contrast to her appearance. The pretty ones look too pretty if given ribbons and frills, the striking ones become grotesque in the more exaggerated of the designs and must be quietened down. One tall girl, named Shiela, is particularly beautiful in movement of body, but the problem of finding just the right things for her to wear took several hours. On the whole, the girls are good-looking and well-behaved, but the duds stick out a mile, and continue to indulge their egos in a variety of unexpected ways.

One dark haired dancer suddenly burst into uncontrollable sobs. 'What's up?' Anne Laune explained that she had 'fallen in love' with a certain blue ball dress. She longed to wear it, whereas I had chosen another for her. 'Well, let's see her in the blue dress.' In spite of a swollen nose and red eyes she looked beautiful. When I told her she could wear it, she broke down again. Some of the confidences are somewhat surprising: 'I have a hip problem.' 'I promise you I will improve my lower portions so that they match up with the upper parts.' 'I'll just have apple juice and cottage cheese and I'll take off ten pounds.' In a hot box situated next to this mass hysteria Gladys Cooper was being fitted for her two new dresses. (I admit they are more becoming to her, much as I liked her erstwhile ball dress.)

The fittings continued until late evening. The appalling heat added to our exertions. Some of the girls were pouring like fountains.

Petch, of the wrinkled forehead, is having a difficult time planning Ascot. 'You've heard we're ordering white gloves for the screen shifters, as they would ruin that white trellis work if they handled it in the usual way. But, you see, not only do we have to get three hundred people on and off the stage, and the West entrance is blocked with the cyclorama, and the women's hats are so large they cannot get through an ordinary doorway, but we have the problem of the horses. Of course, we cannot have thoroughbreds; they are nearly always blind, and so trained to win that, no matter where they are, they run straight in front of themselves: heaven knows what would happen if they came on the set among all these people! Somehow we'll have to have a clear run through for them. These are just some of our problems, but so far we are only two days behind schedule, and we hope to pick up somewhere along the line.'

I went to see the nylon material that is to represent the grass lawns at Ascot. It is a beautiful colour, but Gene warned me, 'You wait until all those lights are put on it, then, with that sheen on, it'll look like snow. We'll have to have men to brush it against the nap between each take'. I refused to be depressed. The Union disputes in abeyance, the tents are being put up and will be worthy of the ungodliest.

On the sound stage the usual 'Silence! No one must move!' Yet Audrey was in high spirits. She could not contain her amusement each time her mouth was filled by Rex with marbles: to get this short scene innumerable 'retakes' were made. When, once more, the camera had to be reloaded and lights switched off, Rex looked at his wrist watch, hoping it was nearly lunch-time.

Whether or not his success in *Cleopatra* is responsible, Rex, whom I have known to be not always easy, has become a changed being – all charm and sweetness. Today he said he'd accede to being photographed by me: this after being as elusive as possible for about three weeks.

6 pm: It is late, and Jean Renoir, the great director who has played a crucial part in the history of the films, and his wife are coming to have dinner tonight, but I chastise myself, and stay on at the studio doing all sorts of extra odd jobs that *could* wait. I even deliver parcels on my way home, and this means motoring out of my usual route. So I return to the hotel only a few moments before the Renoirs arrive. We discuss Hollywood and its lack of flavour today, and the current fashion for kitchenette films made in antiseptic colour displaying the bright brassy hair and freckles of Doris Day. This, sad as it seems to me, is what the American film public wants. But where is the impact of the early pictures which were undoubtedly the great days of Hollywood? With silent movies a tremendous creative talent burgeoned: their inventiveness has never been surpassed. Chaplin, with the crude material at hand, produced works of art. It was a primitive art, 'but primitive art is never bad' said Renoir. When have you seen bad early-Greek sculpture, or cave painting or medieval tapestry? It is only when realism becomes all important, or people have learnt how to do something the wrong way, that art disappears. Before pancromatic film was invented the face, simplified with the black eyes and mouth, became part of a convention the

25 Eliza arriving at the Ball

The Embassy Waltz

28 Eliza

29 'On the street where you live'

30 & 31 'Fine feathers'

32 Higgins has the last word

effect of which was stylish. The studios of Hollywood today use well-tried formulae but concentrate on the perfecting of the technique: the result is that poetry goes out where 'the girl next door' comes in. We agreed that too much money and too many stars are bad for a picture. Above all, too much talk about what is going to be done rather than imaginative action. One must always open the door to chance – and the impromptu. The cinema, more than the theatre, creates its greatest effect by the spontaneous. Fellini's films are glorified charades, and the unexpected is always present in a way that could never be planned. Antonioni, too, knows the dramatic value of the transient, ephemeral fluke.

Before television an enormous, insatiable public had to be fed movies each week. It mattered little what entertainment it was given, for there were always uncritical hordes ready to devour any rubbish. Many of the bigger films that were produced were artificial, well-devised and technically superb pieces of craftsmanship. If they could not be considered works of art they were good commercial enterprises. Today, however, the movie-going public has diminished and has become so critical that, in view of the competition of television, the studios are driven to producing spectacular pictures in the Cecil B. de Mille tradition. As Christopher Isherwood remarked, 'Hollywood is reduced to making masterpieces'.

But not only is Hollywood disinclined to make small pictures in the European technique on a small budget, but it is difficult for it to do so. The effect of such rigid Union rules is to hamstring the Producer. So many electricians to cope with the lights, so many prop-men, hairdressers, stand-ins, etc., etc., etc., are regulations on each film with the result that the budget becomes overloaded. Perhaps Hollywood may be saved by using the technique employed in the making of television films. By their very essence they have to be done cheaply and quickly: in many technical ways, such as the use of colour without emulsion, the viewing of the effects instantaneously on a monitor, and the immediate putting on to tape of the desired effect, so much time and expense will be cut that it may even be possible to make spontaneous experiments and to take risks without the crushing knowledge that overheads are mounting.

The Renoirs have the quality of sympathy that makes one feel at home in their company. With them I am spiritually at ease and

I realize how rare are evenings so glowing with sensitivity and stimulus.

Betsy, my secretary, was saying into the telephone, 'He is just coming in now'. The indefatigable and indestructible Anne Laune already had another group of girls rigged out in Ascot clothes for my inspection.

If I had had time to be depressed today, I would have been dunched at the sight of some of our most treasured dresses now

filled to capacity with human flesh. The costumes that had looked so stylish on the model-stands were slightly creased, yet with mountains bulging tightly where girdles were proving inadequate, or lumps showed the intersection of suspenders. Worse! Leah's fantastic concoctions were being worn at the wrong angle by hard-bitten women with flat faces like *meringues*. No, this will never do! There is surely still time to change this tough, evil-eyed, slot-mouthed lot. Hollywood *must* be able to supply pretty girls.

The morning hours spent ricocheting between Wardrobe, Hairdressing and the Still Gallery. Here I was taking the pictures of flowers for the backgrounds for the 'Credits', and hoping also to lure Rex Harrison from the sound stage. Luck was on my side. I caught Rex at the right moment. 'Would you come across now?' 'What shall I wear?' 'Anything.' 'Really? Doesn't it matter?' 'Nothing matters so long as you get in front of the camera.'

In ten minutes we took a remarkable number of pictures of the old boy, and he was delighted – until suddenly 'danger' flashed. Then he complained, 'I don't want to get tired doing this during a day's work'. Perhaps, fortunately, he was immediately recalled to the set.

A posse of models were then being photographed in Ascot hats when Audrey tracked me down here to discuss her ballroom coiffure. She had been thinking about how to achieve the effect of my latest sketch. 'Shouldn't that pinnacle of curls be a separate solid bit that can be put on each morning?' 'Yes, we could get Max Factor's to supply a special hair piece.' Just to prove the efficiency of a great film studio, grey-faced Petch came in, a short while later, to say this hair piece must be ordered right away – 'Only three weeks to go before that scene will be shot, and tests must be made beforehand.'

'But, Petch, it's all right talking about hair, but where's the bloody Ballroom? I haven't even seen a plank of wood yet.' 'Oh, they're clearing Stage 20 already, and it'll be soon put up: don't worry – it'll be ready in time.'

Meanwhile, more women ready in Hairdressing for my criticism, and out it came. 'This is much too exaggerated! This is too rock-like for words, add more, take away . . .' By now, more girls are ready to be seen in Wardrobe: others are not. I am impatient. 'Sorry, girls: I'm coming in here right away, so if anyone doesn't want to be seen naked, get into the other room or cover yourselves up!' The glimpses of girls, stark naked except for an enormous hat, are like the covers of *La Vie Parisienne*.

One or two of my 'bad pennies' have again edged their way in and, of course, they have cultivated to perfection the technique of being difficult. By degrees, my compassion for even the most pathetic of them has worn off, and I realize how quickly a dictator can unlearn the humane habits.

Wednesday, 2 October

If you go on doing anything long enough, however, unpleasant, it becomes routine. The arrival of twenty-five more women, each to be fitted out in two sets of costumes, continued twice a day. Having been given the right dress and hat, they would be sent to Hairdressing. Then for me the judging.

There are so many possibilities of inter-Departmental messages being misconstrued that Joe Hiatt has arranged for me to have a 'Co-Ordinator'. This person's job is to convey to each Department concerned my wishes about how the performers are to be presented. 'Nobody told me!' is the usual wail. Now a very

bright, gipsy-like authoress in her own right, Gerda Roberson, is to be the Co-Ordinator between Wardrobe, Props, Hairdressing and Makeup. 'It's a tough job!' Gerda girded her loins and went into battle. She called, 'I've told them about the crystal necklaces, and all the Ball ladies to be painted pink and white with no eye-liner, but there are some hairdo's you'd better come over and see right away'. When I arrived at Hairdressing Gerda laughed, 'I wanted you to see the one with sausage curls, like a Restoration comedy belle. I just wanted to see your reaction'. It was a very quick one – 'Off with all that nonsense!' No sooner shouted than done. The hairdressers, I am glad to say, have hardly any fight left in them: they have become obedient. I came away with a wry smile on my beastly face.

It was late at the studio: Audrey, George and I left simultaneously but separately. George said, 'We have really earned our money today'. Audrey grimaced and did an imitation of an octogenarian. 'I'm beginning to feel my age. I used never to get tired, but these last two weeks . . .' She looked as fresh as a dewdrop, and only a softness in her eyes gave any indication of fatigue.

On the stage 'The Rain In Spain' ground on. Although George considered that at last a perfect 'take' had been achieved the musical expert, Friml, asked for another. 'Why another?' 'Because it's a bit rubbery,' said Friml. Audrey has sufficient technique to be able to emote any number of times with the identical delicate spontaneity. George remembered. 'On that "take" you did the second line better than ever before.'

Rex was a trifle tetchy today. I asked him if he was free to look at his photographs. Euphemistically, but with a good deal of bite in his voice, he said, 'I'm afraid I'm just about to do a little spot of work'. (This consisted of feeding Audrey her lines.) When the scene was finished, George Cukor asked if I would like to have a photograph of the scene. I was somewhat dumbfounded, since I have come to feel that to snap the camera on the set is in the nature of an indecency. In fact, it has given me quite a complex. Yet to take photographs of the production is part of the work for which I am contracted. Not only that: it is only natural that I should wish to record, in my own way, the work that I have done, particularly upon the exquisite leading lady for every infinitesimal detail of whose appearance I am responsible.

Delighted with the change of events I asked Rex if he would sit with Audrey, and he plumped himself on a seat which was so low that it showed him in an unflattering lumped-up position while Audrey towered above him. 'Won't you sit on the arm of the sofa?' 'No, old cock, you get someone else to pose for a backview.' I moaned with genuine surprise. 'But I wanted a profile.' 'They've not lit me for that profile,' said Rex, as George Cukor roared with amusement.

But no need to fret. I took the opportunity to photograph Audrey by her sweet self. Moreover there were other things to occupy my mind. Limey, the 'prop' man (who always salutes me like the 1914 soldier that he is), wanted to order fifty more pairs of race glasses. 'Go ahead.' I inspected the servants' hair: they are supposed to have been woken up in the middle of the night and must appear rather frowsty. Then a crowd of about a hundred women arrived, and I had glumly to walk down the line, like the Duke of Clarence, inspecting them. To have to pass over all but a fraction of those that had taken the trouble to come here used to be a penance of embarrassment and humiliation for me. But I am now getting accustomed to meeting the stares, pleading or resentful, and passing on. Today, having run the gauntlet a fourth time, as requested to satisfy the Guild, I was even able to indulge in badinage with a few of the poor outcasts.

The pettifogging details continue. Geoff submitted flannel for the pyjamas of the butler and footmen. The Director wished to see the ring that Eliza throws into the fire. 'Too important,' he said, 'try and get an antique one.' 'But it has to be triplicated!' Seven dowagers were trussed up for the two scenes of Ascot and the Ball. The barrel is scraped now; only a few dresses left.

So throughout the day: so it has been for many months. Is it any wonder that I have no mentality?

Thursday, 3 October

Visitors appeared from the outside world today. This is always a relief. Anyone who is not bound by contract to this project seems to have wings. The local *Vogue* lady was a refreshment, and when I saw Hubert Givenchy it was a forgotten whiff of Paris. He is gentlemanly and good, so quietly behaved, unhurried and civilized. It was a pleasure to show him all the stuff that we've stacked up in Wardrobe. He was amazed at such detail, and said, 'What a work! It's as much as half a dozen collections!'

Audrey was describing to the *Vogue* lady the effect my dresses made on her. She said they were somewhat static in complement to the hats which were like birds or which looked as if they were 'taking-off', and they gave movement to the face.

Just as I was about to scram for home the indestructible Anne called: 'Wait! There are ten more girls in ball-dresses waiting for you to see them.' Of course there were! By now we have got down to my least favourite dresses. Then Audrey called me to say she had been thinking over her statement about the static clothes, and thought she would prefer to say that I had 'done a *Pygmalion*' and given life to something static. She is always calm and precise and business-like.

Cukor called me to the set to talk about who should replace Fritzi Massary. Tentatively I suggested a certain well-known local celebrity. 'She has no real distinction. Did you see that picture of her buttonholing the Queen and Princess Margaret when they were children? The surprise and disgust on their faces!' I suggested a mutual friend, an amateur lady. 'She would not know how to walk!' 'Would you object to amateurs?' 'Not necessarily.' Simultaneously, we suggested Bina Rothschild, a grey-haired lady of ineffable distinction who, for the past twenty years, has lived in a house which she has endowed with her native Austrian atmosphere in Mandeville Canyon. 'Go and ask her if she would do it.' Bina reacted in just the way we hoped. The deep Austrian voice reverberated over the telephone: 'I think it might be fun!' No nonsense about whether she could do the part, never having been on the stage, Bina arrived later that day on the set. She is as tall as Fritzi is small, but, even more important, she is thrilled to be given the part of the Queen of Transylvania. Gerda opined: 'That bit of casting was an inspiration.' The lunch interval was spent organizing Bina's jewellery; the high dog collar, a three winged tiara, a three strand diamond necklace the size of walnuts, and taking her measurements so that the Parma violet ball dress could be sent off immediately to have a thousand dollars of embroidery worked into it.

Monday, 7 October

Six o'clock call to be on the set for test shots of the Ascot scene. Today the freeway was as crowded at this early hour as for the evening exodus.

Hairdressing had done a good job: Leah's hats really 'worked': final fittings to the dresses had made all the difference, and the mass effect of the magpie girls was extremely *chic*: this was a triumph of concentrated efforts over matter.

As for the Ascot set, it is the cleanest, most airy thing. Consisting, as it does, entirely of linen and painted wood, it must be one of the cheapest sets Warner's have ever made. The varying whites, pale greens, and greys make a clear background for the dresses, and the hanging baskets of hydrangeas, for whose existence an agonizing battle had been fought and won, are one-hundred per cent successful.

Generally I go around with a harassed expression on my face, but today was really an exception, and I tried consciously to enjoy the lighthearted atmosphere. Cukor was directing on Stage Two ('I Could Have Danced All Night'), and the second unit was under the direction of Gene. I was permitted to take photographs. Even though the principals were not on hand the extras provided me with many opportunities for interesting compositions. I suddenly felt as if a gentle spring zephyr was blowing among the trellises of Ascot.

Tuesday, 8 October

Felled with acute laryngitis. To be voiceless in Bel-Air is indeed to be plagued. Without recourse to telephone help, too low for reading, this is a quick way to feel extremely lonely. It is perhaps fortunate that I still have to cope with problems at the studio. Messages came through to quicken the pulse.

Eleanor arrived with a sheaf of papers on which I had to write down the answers to various enquiries. Things are humming: they are going to push forward the day of shooting Ascot: it seems a day and a half has been made up on the schedule, and now there is an unholy rush to complete the staircase, anteroom and ballroom by next Wednesday.

Thursday, 10 October

The first real day of shooting Ascot. My presence was essential, but still no croak could emerge from my throat, so I went about with a notice pinned to my coat: 'Laryngitis, sorry cannot talk.' In this smog-ridden vicinity this is a commonplace illness, and no one seemed surprised at my enforced silence.

In the middle of the crowds of racegoers Audrey (who is known by the Frank Sinatra group as 'The Princess') appeared to be tested in her ballroom dress and coiffure. Never has she more lived up to her name, and never was her allure more obvious than now as she smiled radiantly or shyly, flickered her eyelids, lowered her lashes, blinked, did all the tricks of allure with enormous assurance. She gyrated in front of the camera while two hundred extras watched. She was vastly entertained that some of them were scrutinizing her through their race glasses.

The glistening ball dress is like ice on trees in Switzerland, and her new coiffure is certainly startling, but I wish I could have prescribed something a little more of the period to which her hairdresser had added style and lightness.

Friday, 11 October

Slept for twelve hours. Still no voice on waking. This gives me cripple complex.

On the Ascot set only a half-strength crowd had been summoned for the dialogue scenes between Rex and others. Audrey, according to the Wardrobe Plot wearing Costume 13 ('Eliza is a success until she forgets herself during race'), was resting on a lounging board. I asked her in dumb crambo if she would come to the side of the set to pose for a photograph while they were arranging the next shot. This she did with pleasure. Buck Hall, the Assistant Director, then asked us not to get in the way of the cleaners who were polishing the floor. 'Could we move down here?' I gesticulated. Buck gave the 'OK' sign. 'You're sure it will be all right here?' I whispered, then nodded my thanks. In pantomime I gave suggestions to Audrey who was posing among the trellis work. Two minutes later Buck Hall returned. 'Would you please not take Audrey off the set.' Without a voice I croaked: 'But you said it would be O.K. here!' 'Mr Cukor doesn't want you to take pictures of Audrey while they are fixing the lights.' 'Then when can I?' I wheezed. 'Mr Cukor does not want you to photograph her on the set during any of her working days.' 'All her days are working days and I have been waiting a month for this opportunity.' Looking very pained, Audrey argued in secret with Buck Hall, who was most anxious that Mr Cukor's sugar should not ferment. For the moment I felt no pain. Audrey said: 'I can't be in the middle of this, but try not to be too upset.' She, meanwhile, smoked a cigarette outside while waiting to be summoned for a long shot of her silent entry to the races. I was later told that it took George Cukor two hours to recover from his displeasure with me enough to continue.

Tuesday, 15 October

Gave instructions about colours of the Ballroom to Gene, and suggestions for the technique of painting the *grisaille* decorations on the *sous-portes* of the anteroom. They should be done in a Condor fan technique, watery and vague. The Embassy staircase is now covered with huge sheets of brown paper, while the delicate ironwork balustrade is being picked out in gold. If only ordinary people could have their houses run up in so short a time! The staircase carpet must be specially dyed a deep burgundy red, and I must choose the type of electric bulbs to be used in the wall brackets and chandeliers. I picked out a large suite of Adam sofas and chairs, and these miraculously will be covered in sea-green *moiré* (to be flown from New York) by the time shooting begins in three days' time. Geoff was awaiting an 'OK' for medals and ribbons for the Ball, and Anne with a fan for Audrey. Other enquiries came from the set: 'What *boutonnières* for the men? Is it all right for Mr Harrison to have a gardenia?'

The policeman at the gate stopped me on my way to the doctor. An urgent request: 'What should be on the table for the "high tea" when the Higgins' household returned from Ascot?' 'If it is really "high", give them shrimps.' Dick from 'Props' then asked. 'Would there be tooth picks with the shrimps?' 'No, but toast.' 'What shape?' I drew triangles of toast and gave the

dimensions 'and put it in a muffin dish.' Later, George Hopkins appeared. 'What sort of a muffin dish?' I did a drawing. 'That shouldn't be difficult to find, but,' he said, 'the chairs for the Embassy Hall will be!' I then went back to the 'Props' Museum and looked at more furniture. Not only does Warner own a great collection of rare pieces that have been bought in the best anti-quaries of Europe, but the copies of English, French, Spanish and Italian pieces of all periods are so extraordinary that they would provoke altercations between curators of museums.

Went to see the tests of the Ascot scene, and glad to think that they are only tests. The camera somehow had reduced everything to a degree of banality. It is as if our opalescent setting had been reproduced by some cheap, coloured picture-postcard process. In spite of all previous tests, the men's coats came out blue, Rex Harrison's face Red Indian, and the subtle graduations of cream and white, over which we had deliberated like philosophers, suddenly became olive drab and beige. 'Oh, this is not a rectified print,' I was told when I moaned in despair.

Hardly anyone was allowed beyond the Cerberus guardian at the entrance to the set. Even Anne Laune, who has been so largely responsible for any costume used in the picture, was forbidden the precincts. Rumours of hyper-tension had reached my stronghold so I steered clear of 'panicville' with a great determination.

Gerda, the co-ordinator, came to report on her liaison work. When I remarked that she was fighting to the death in the most noble of causes, she replied that she felt she was calling on the homes of the Medicis at the time of their greatest power. When she asked me how I felt, I croaked, 'Could be worse,' and she said, 'I see, pleasure being the absence of pain.' However, on the side of pleasure, a note of eulogy arrived from Jack Warner for the Ascot set and Audrey's costume in particular.

I suppose it is the accumulation of tightly-packed days, weeks and months that gradually has brought upon me this heavy weight of exhaustion. I can now keep at bay only at shorter intervals this general feeling of depletion.

Each dew-glittering morning when I set off, clean and tingling, after the swim and shower, I feel re-born: there is a joyous spirit of adventure about getting on to the freeway in this powerful

new car in which one can drive one's foot down hard on the accelerator as one streaks along these conveniently deserted ribbons of tarmac.

It is always agreeable to be greeted in my rooms by my secretary, Betsy Cox, and her reassuring smile which semaphores to me the fact that of all the chores needing immediate attention, none is likely to prove disagreeable. (It is only if her nose twitches as she hands me a slip of paper that I know I must brace myself for a difficult interview.)

The element of surprise keeps each smiling morning quite different from another: at this early hour everyone is sparkling and full of zest, and work seems to be smoothly done. However, by midday my energy is beginning to sag a little, and the mind surreptitiously wanders in the direction of tomato or grapefruit juice, cottage cheese and salad. Pangs of hunger denote the turning of the hands of the clock, and soon starts the inevitable decline in vitality. Never before have I been more conscious of the revitalising effect of food. (Not that one can eat great quantities in this climate. It is strange how an Englishman, accustomed to a substantial lunch, soon adapts himself to the light Californian fare.)

But, while most people on the lot enjoy the midday break in

the company of their fellow humans in the deep-bellied *bonhomie* of the Commissary, I seek refuge in my own room. The tray, brought in by the Philippine messenger boy, is dispensed with in record time, so that, with ears plugged with wax pellets, a few extra minutes of siesta can be snatched on the Biedermayer sofa. My batteries recharged by half-an-hour's oblivion, the afternoon is embarked upon with the anticipation one feels on seeing the curtain rise for the second act of a play. But the post-prandial stretch takes on a different tempo and a more mellow mood from that of the morning, and it dictates its own form of work. Perhaps it is not such a good time for the more creative processes; this is a period for decisions and supervision in guiding the development of work already set in motion. As the afternoon progresses, the unexpected snags that have arisen during the day in many other departments descend upon one's head. 'I have a little problem here,' says a crestfallen friend bearing a book of lincrusta patterns. One learns that the manufacturers of formica glass are unable to supply the windows in Wimpole Street as hoped for, Max Adrian has been forbidden to leave the Chichester Festival and must be replaced in the ballroom so the shooting schedule is being altered, and an Aubusson carpet, forty foot by fifty-three, must be found by nine o'clock tomorrow morning.

By five o'clock I sense that the sacking is beginning to split and all the sand is running out of my body. It is an interesting and not altogether unpleasant sensation: one marvels that it can go on so long at increasing ratio, and that one can continue to motivate.

But I know from past experience that this is a dangerous period. It is quite possible that decisions I am making now will have been arrived at with insufficient patience or care. During the night I will begin to realize this, and my anxiety accumulates until I have, early next morning, been able to reconsider my verdict or countermand an instruction.

I should learn that the moment a certain degree of fatigue has been reached it is necessary for me forthwith to escape before I have cost the company a large sum of money by a mistake. But this is often an impossibility for it is inevitably at the thirteenth hour that someone arrives with an SOS.

Yet what a fine moment it is when, with the welter of the day's work behind one, one again takes to the wheel of the motor car! Unfortunately the return journey is not like the early morning adventure. The traffic on the freeway is at its most concentrated: fumes and heat continue to drain the oxygen from the air and the remaining energy from every limb: the evening sun pricks into every pore. The journey takes twice as long. Always some exasperation in the form of a breakdown, or a maniac driver risking his life and yours for a ten yard advancement in the impatient stream of traffic. At this hour the cares of the studio fall on one in retrospect. What has the day's work been about? Was it worth that battle? One's mind is jaundiced by fatigue: nothing seems as it should be. One switches on the car radio, but all programmes seem designed to encourage one's exasperation. Never mind! Try, try, try to preserve yourself in peace until that glorious moment – surely not too far off now – of returning to the cool darkness of one's room, to finding the messages fixed in the mesh door, the sudden new interests, and the drink tray ... It is now that the Englishman regrets the leisurely hot soak. A shower, alternately hot and cold, is invigorating, but it is at such times that one longs to be horizontal, and however unattractive it may seem to the most immaculate of Americans, an Englishman enjoys lying in his own suds and muck.

I cannot pretend that each evening on returning from the studio I have preserved my strength for the morrow by dining in bed, or even making an early night of it. Two solitary evenings alone with a book during the working week are essential to me, but I have a curiosity to see every aspect of Hollywood life, and there are hospitable friends with welcome invitations – and some of them show foreign films in their houses on a screen which mysteriously descends in front of the Cézannes and Renoirs. Who can resist?

Once a week I have dined with Christopher Isherwood. Refreshed and eager, after a short respite in my Bel-Air lair, I have often said to myself, as I motored towards his most pleasant house overlooking the Bay of Santa Monica, that the evening in front of me would be a completely happy one, that nowhere in the world could one enjoy more agreeable company than here in this sympathetic atmosphere with the talk that invigorates. Here there is no need of explanation; here is the understanding that inspires, the wit that stimulates. The host, shy at first, gradually warms to the evening, and, no doubt encouraged as we all are by the good Southern dishes and glowing wine, displays in verbal brilliance his belief in friendliness and goodness, and his scorn for the false and ungodly; in short, values which through all the vicissitudes through which he has passed, from his early days in the decadence of Berlin in the twenties to his stints as a writer of scenarios, punching a studio clock, in spite of all the vulgarity surrounding him, have remained constant in him.

The glow of the evening continues long after one has left Christopher's house, and one realizes that the return journey in the car has passed without one's having been conscious of making the half-hour trip back to a more prosaic, and certainly less innocent, world.

It is only then that the hands of the clock have advanced so that one has left disastrously inadequate time to build up one's forces for the 'Big Push' tomorrow.

Gene appeared with the model for Mrs Higgins' house. This is the last set to be made. Thank God it looks excellent, full of ingenious nooks and crannies and very 'Voysey' and 'English arts and crafts'. It should be amusing, and a real change.

Friday, 18 October

I was surprised when Audrey called to ask if I would come and check her Ball appearance for she was about to make her entrance down the Higgins' staircase. Golly! The production is really moving apace!

Audrey looked cool and immaculate as usual, but there was an essentially modern look to the hair. I tentatively suggested: 'Perhaps this isn't the moment to mention it, but don't you think that a little softness at the temples?' 'Oh, but I like the clean look.' Audrey knows when she looks her best, and certainly this is the scene in which it is more important to her to look absolutely stunning than it is to preserve an authentic period flavour.

Tuesday, 22 October

Today was the 'Big Push'. All the women for whom we have made Ascot dresses were called in, over a hundred and fifty of them. Hairdressers had to start at dawn, but as each woman has already been 'established' (has had her photograph taken showing every angle of her hair style, the angle of the hat, her jewellery and her props) there should have been no reason for me to supervise: who's being funny?

While in the barber's shop a message from the set: would I join Jack Warner and Fritz Loewe on the Ascot set. Fritz, unable to stay away from the activities any longer, had flown from Palm Springs to see how his deathless songs had been screened. Jack and he had just sat in a projection room watching a rough cut of the first part of our picture. Their enthusiasm gave a tremendous lift to the cast. Meanwhile, the race scene was about to start. All on-lookers were being banished out of sight of the action, but I

stayed firmly watching proceedings from behind a lamp. George told Jack Warner to move away, but Jack, with a big grin on his face, said: 'No, you're not moving me from here.' George bit his lip in acutest embarrassment.

Later, Jack took Fritz and me to see the rest of the film to date. When Audrey sang 'I Could Have Danced All Night', the three of us, alone in the dark theatre, burst into spontaneous applause. Fritz, euphoric, and demonstrative as only the Viennese can be, kissed both Jack and myself.

Wednesday, 23 October

Another 'Big Push' – one hundred and fifty women to be hair-dressed, made up, bejewelled, clothed and cloaked for the arrival at the Embassy. Comparative calm reigned when I arrived, for many of the women had been worked upon since dawn. Now the personal touch was necessary. I got busy wrecking and re-making hair styles, pulling at wigs, pulling at real hair. A few of the hairdressers aghast, but that could not be helped. At one point I overheard a distraught lady telephoning: 'Send ten more hair stylists tomorrow. It's for pretty period hair-dos.' I wondered if, from her cryptic SOS, we would find our ladies coiffed as Cleopatra, Joan of Arc, Marie Antoinette, or Christina Rossetti? My fight with the hairdressers continued into the afternoon when I wanted to change some particularly inept coiffure, and I was told, 'It's already been established in a shot and can't be changed,' or, 'You passed that yesterday!' But I pit my eye and memory against hairdressers.

Anne Laune was smiling with pleasure when Leah and I set to work, applying the head-dresses that were to give the finishing touches to the ladies.

Bina Rothschild's warmth of humanity and cosiness of manner is very much in contrast to the brittle façade of some others in our cast. As she sat being coiffed as the Queen, Bina gave an aura of distinction and warm-heartedness to the entire building. Her tiara affixed, we went to the Wardrobe for the Queen's embroidered dress to be fitted. In her Parma violet and silver, with the pale green Order across her bosom, Bina recaptures all the romance of an old photograph by Lallie Charles.

Thursday, 24 October

Mort Lichter's infinitely sad voice on the telephone. Yes, he'd got me permission to take photographs on the set this morning, under the same conditions as the other 'still' men. But be careful, he warned me, as the atmosphere is pretty explosive down there: he'd already had his share of being bawled at.

The climate on the staircase set was tropical – perhaps any moment now the storm would break – but would it clear the air? Naturally, one of the few girls who was placed close in to camera was worthy for a position only in the far distance. Uncanny how those responsible for picking the girls for prominence have an unfailing eye for the dud. When one tries to interfere by sending to oblivion the girl-Cyclops with the pear-shaped nose, there is such a to-do that one wonders if more feelings and emotions are not involved than one would care to envisage.

They were doing the crowd arriving at the Embassy with Eliza taking off her cloak and, with much trepidation, mounting the staircase to be greeted by her hostess. It is a great moment in the story but, because of 'retakes' and without any build-up, here in front of the cameras it seemed to be lacking in emotion; in fact, appearances were cold.

I mounted a perilously tall ladder and clicked from aloft onto a mimed scene. Mort Lichter, looking sadder and more parroty than ever, warned me that the director had ruled that no pictures might be taken during a rehearsal even though the sound track was not being used and the click of the camera would not be disturbing. In between 'takes' the scene was invaded by 'prop' men in Honolulu shirts polishing the marble floors, and equally garishly garbed dressers, not content to leave well alone, doing their endless titivating. When the scene had been shot six times the 'still' men were given a few seconds in which to register the past event. Of course, photographs are not even an important detail of a $17,000,000 project.

But not only the 'still' photographers seem to be bugbears: high tension has become an integral element in the atmosphere on the set in which this picture is being made. I have begun to feel like a trespasser on the sets that I have designed.

The laugh of the morning came when Buck Hall shouted into the mike: 'Quiet! We've tried to be nice to you all, but if . . .' Cukor backed him up: 'Can't you have the *civility* to be quiet?' In contrast to the hysteria surrounding the Director and his assistants, or maybe on account of it, is the boredom and casualness of some of the actors, most of the extras and the indulgent technical staff.

Rex was in good humour as, time and again, up and down the staircase, he had to walk. Yet another 'take', so up and down once more. Marvellously svelte in his tail coat in a housemaid's voice he confided: 'Oh, my feet! These stairs are killing me!'

Thursday, 24 October

Darkness now arrives early in the afternoon, and the nights become a bit nippy. But the trees remain the same as ever and do not seem to lose their leaves, and there is little to show what month of the year we are in.

The daily rushes are often somewhat exasperating: Before 'cutting', the extraneous always assumes importance. As soon as one settles down to enjoy a few moments of consecutive dialogue an abrupt voice from outer space interrupts: 'Good, very good, print that.' One cannot but be disturbed by seeing the clapperboard man wearing Joseph's shirt of many colours and the equally garishly garbed dressers who become featured players and wreck all efforts of keeping the palette under control. The latest Ascot scenes done by the second unit show clear whites, and the complexions of the women are pearly and opalescent: for that I am grateful. Yet somehow it is always the toughest, brashest extra that comes within close camera range. However, criticisms of various groupings are at this stage unhelpful, for one is seeing minute particles of film that are designed to build up into a whole.

Thursday, 31 October

Hopkins came in to show me upholstery materials for the Mrs Higgins set which is now being built and, this complete, my work on the sets will be finished.

They are now hanging the *art nouveau* wallpaper. The plans for the grotto have become too baroque, and I asked Gene to countermand the shell work, as this would have been too rococo and out of keeping with Fabian taste.

The entrance of the Queen into the Ballroom was most impressive. Bina behaved with just the right amount of shy gaucherie and innate pride: her gangling carriage, her off-hand authority and shy naturalness are authentic. Every jewel belongs to her, every wave of her hair is evocative of the real thing.

Audrey was very friendly and, daring displeasure from higher quarters, even looked into my camera lens from the vantage point of her chair rest. Buck Hall commented that the crank of my camera was noisy, and must be attended to.

A great part of my life has been spent in the United States. New York has become my second winter home, and I am no stranger to Hollywood. Having started out as an enthusiastic sun and star-gazing sightseer, it was a golden day when I graduated to become part of the working colony. Making the film *Gigi* with Minelli was an utterly congenial business.

But, on this particular journey, remaining in one specific place, leading a super-imposed existence for so great a length of time,

it surprises me to feel so much more foreign than during any previous visit. Never before have I realized quite so definitely the schism between certain English and Americans.

Hollywood is not typical of this country. Admittedly it would be a laugh to consider myself a typical Englishman, and my reactions must be particular to me. But not only do I find that I cannot readily make myself understood by word of mouth (and certainly my handwriting is indecipherable for those brought up to write in a depersonalized copper-plate), but I know that my whole point of view creates bafflement – I am looked upon as something as curious and unaccountable as the unicorn.

Probably the people I see in other big cities of the United States are Europeans working here, or are Europeanized Americans, so naturally there is a closer affinity; but even among the reputed Anglophiles here I have never before been so conscious of the difference in attitude of mind. Much of this is refreshing. That 'outgoing' sense of fellowship is flattering and welcoming. 'Come in, relax and make yourself at home.' The ebb and flow of conversation is made as painless and easy as can be. The friendliness may not be very deep-seated but it is genuine none the less. I am grateful for it, and I am lucky enough to have made one or two lasting friendships.

But, after a while, I ask myself why is it that here so few people indulge in the art of conversation, do not throw ideas back and forth, avoid argument or listening, and, instead of sharpening their wits, have recourse to the ready-made wisecrack? What is it that I find lacking here? What is the ingredient that manifests itself as being English – and without which I am unable to fulfil myself?

At home there are plenty of us who, however, aged, have never attained maturity, who have chips on both shoulders, who hold down their jobs by avoiding issues, and whenever possible 'passing the buck'. We all like to be praised, often by fools, but especially by the people we admire, and we can all put on blinkers when it comes to one's shortcomings.

But however escapist our wishes it is difficult sooner or later to avoid reality on some level. Yet here it seems that after so many labour-saving devices comes thought-saving: Talk resolves itself into a series of *clichés* so that the brain, for want of an opponent to pit against, becomes desiccated in the smog. Any juxtaposition of words that does not strike the ear with the sound of familiarity becomes a jolt: 'What's he saying? Is he kidding me?' is the first reaction; often misunderstanding turns to resentment.

It is when suddenly one talks to a fellow traveller that one realizes the relief at not having to explain – when one's efforts, however crude, at communication do not fall on fallow ground.

A somewhat confounding experience: Intending to show off to a visitor from outside the various sets for which I have acquired the same affection as for an old friend I discovered that already the ballroom, ante-room and Embassy staircase had been denuded of their light fittings, furniture and 'props' before being dismantled and stored away in pieces. But the glorious white *treillage* world of Ascot had not only been torn down but (so I had been informed) somewhat ghoulishly taken away and burned.

Three weeks to go before my contract is up. Morning spent painting Jeremy Brett as Freddie. Started badly, but with great effort got through to near success. I realized the end of my visit was in sight when Stanley Fleicher of the Art Department came to say he had heard I was leaving, and would I return to him any of the 'artists' materials' I had not used.

An even more definite feeling of departure was produced with a cable from New York from Jack Warner thanking me for my contribution to the picture. He has been a noble support all along the line.

Monday, 11 November

Audrey has no spare time to pose for a painting, so suggested that, if I liked, she would sit during her lunch interval. A great effort to slash paint on canvas while she ate her salad and talked of the sad things that had happened to her over the weekend. Her son had been ill with a temperature of 103°, the canary had flown away, and somebody had stolen from her mobile dressing-room a bag with her diamond wedding ring in it. She said that every morning she had been getting up at 5.30 am, and this had continued for six months. 'No matter how you slice it, you just don't get enough sleep, even if you go to bed at 9.30 pm.' She has an extraordinary discipline, and this she calls upon so that she is able to endure until the last day of shooting. If a picture were to continue three days longer than she is geared for, total collapse would be inevitable. It is thus with many of the leading actors working under the merciless pace of all studios. My painting just passable under the circumstances.

Audrey went back to the slipper-throwing scene.

Monday, 18 November

Mel Ferrer called me to say that after all these early mornings Audrey was completely depleted, had no further resistance, and was taking three days off to sleep and rest, and be treated by a doctor. She would give three extra days after her contract expiress However, she hoped to be back to see me before I leave.

Rex suddenly appeared. 'I hear you're leaving. Have you finished with me?' If not, he would pose for a drawing or a photograph any time. Of course, this led to many false alarms in which everything was prepared for the appearance of Rex, but he did not, as the phrase has it, 'show'. However, he promised he would be available the following morning.

Rex was on the set singing 'Why Can't A Woman Be Like a Man?', but the microphone worn in his tie was giving difficulties. The technical side still rules all. (Recently, a morning's work with Jeremy and Audrey was spoilt by the camera suddenly giving a 'colour wobble', so that once more they had to do a complicated dance routine.)

Thursday

Mrs Higgins' house looks like a Kate Greenaway-Walter Crane version of *art nouveau*. I was so elated with the day-nursery effects that I insisted upon registering them on colour film immediately. This added to the already vast back-log of work on sensitized paper and gelatine that has to be finished before tomorrow's departure.

Meanwhile, Rex had made another appointment for his sketch. The easel had been set up in his dressing-room adjoining the Wimpole Street set (where, this morning, crowds of extras disguised as pedestrians and taxi drivers, etc., had congregated). But Rex was conversing with the Director in the porch of Dr Gottfried's house, and it was not for me to disturb them. When I returned to the set an hour later I was told that Rex had gone for the day. However, I caught him on his way out and, much against his will, dragged him to my room. Once I started painting he was flattered. He is like a changeable schoolboy. He watched the painting with growing interest, and I must say that, without time to realize its faults, the result pleased me. It was, in fact, more alive than that of Hyde-White, who had given me un-limited time yet whose picture had become muddy and *travaillé*. Rex even submitted to being photographed. It was all so easy now that he was in the palm of one's hand! Yet it had been impossible to arrange. For weeks the Publicity Department had tried in vain to make appointments.

Someone once said that only a weak sentence needs for emphasis the word 'damn'. By this token there are many of the older generation in the film colony today whose conversation signifies little – consisting, as it does, of the very limited stream of every four-letter word in scatology. Is it that people feel that in order to be of a 'good-guy norm', to be 'on terms' and 'make their way' with others without showing superiority, they must have recourse to the bad language of the fourth form? It has been explained, or even pardoned, as 'a Hollywood convention'. I tried to investigate this subject, and asked a man who has yearnings towards erudition if this was inspired by fear of being different from the custodian, a conscientious effort at conformity at its lowest level. He replied, 'But surely it's the only way to talk!' A comedienne, whose language was known to be particularly rough, explained her attitude more succinctly by saying: 'Anybody who don't use the word "shit" is deceitful.'

Certain 'way out' humorists today have been jailed for the obscenity of their jokes. But theirs is an effort to break down convention, and to shock, that is part of the 'Beat' point of view. But there is no shock value in this 'get together' repetition of lavatory-wall graffiti which, with over-usage, becomes like an attack of hiccups. It may be that the foul-mouthed are merely insecure and are one of the few relics of immaturity in a Hollywood that, for all its present-day difficulties, has become adult.

Groups of hopeful sightseers on the lot are a common and rather sorry sight. They trundle doggedly after some enterprising delivery-boy who has been given the thankless job of showing these footsore travellers around in the hope of catching sight of a star. But their chances of success are limited: it is easier to pass through the eye of a needle than to enter a 'Closed Set' in which Frank Sinatra or Dean Martin are having a good time, or Bette Davis is enjoying a tantrum.

Presumably those crazily-dressed old dames who wave pamphlets at the motors rushing by on Sunset Boulevard occasionally find a purchaser willing to pay fifty cents for Greer Garson's address in Bel-Air, but celebrity hunting in Hollywood is all rather small beer in comparison to what it was in the days when Valentino's 'Falcon's Lair' was a wild, wonderful eerie, when electric bulbs were encased in the coloured glass grapes of Mae Murray's Spanish bedroom, and Jeanette McDonald lived in a mansion decorated with Monte Carlo *pâtisseries*.

It is not merely that I myself am no longer a fervent stargazer (or that I have found proximity breeds disenchantment), but in this respect also, Hollywood has changed. Not that it is dead – as we have heard and read so often: a great number of films are still being made here, and will always continue to be made, and television entertainment has become a thriving product to help keep the studios busy. But the era when Hollywood was the centre of the world's headlines is over. Not only the foreign stars, but many Americans, rush back to Switzerland to snatch their savings away from the Californian Income Tax collector. Many Hollywood actors make their pictures in Italy, Spain or Scandinavia. Few of them keep up large houses in California. The former 'mansions' are divided into apartments.

And what enjoyment could today's fans acquire from gazing upon the neo-Georgian villa-residence leased to stars before returning to their tax-free address in Zurich?

Hollywood (if that is the generic term one can still use to comprise Los Angeles, Beverly Hills, Bel-Air, Brentwood and the San Fernando Valley) is more alive than it ever was: estate values and rent go up each month as the influx of permanent residents to California increases at a rate of seventeen hundred a day. Its life has become more cultured: every suburb has its own excellent picture galleries, bookshop and antiquaires, extremely *chic* sports clothes and interior-decoration shops, and the level of taste has risen high on the thermometer. The women wear quiet, impeccable little dresses: the rich behave circumspectly and know how to entertain: culture is an available commodity. Everything has become extremely civilized, respectable and, perhaps, a bit more dull.

But it is big business and the scientific laboratories that are thriving – oil, engineering, chemicals, machinery, processed foods and the making of automobiles are of prime importance, and nuclear physicists and scientists congregate here from all parts of the world. (The 'Brain Drain' from Britain comes gushing out here.) The motion picture industry has fallen from being the *raison d'être* of this community to becoming of minor note.

The change has brought about many great advantages: for the first time in its history Los Angeles is developing a civic sense. Early movie tycoons were known as the 'fur trappers' – like their namesakes who, when they had hunted the otters of Northern California until they became extinct, left the vicinity without a

legacy of any kind. Southern California has sprouted several little oases of culture, of well-endowed, delightful small universities.

The tarnished glitter of Hollywood is superseded by the golden dawn of the new Los Angeles. Today's millionaires have given, and continue to give, towards bigger and better museums, medical centres, concert auditoria and theatres. The scale on which building is planned at the UCLA* is Babylonian. Los Angeles is fast developing into one of the richest and greatest centres of the arts of America. (Already it has exceeded in scope and riches its cultural neighbour, San Francisco.)

Yet the many varieties of people who, for one reason or another, have made South California their home, can hardly yet be called a community: there is no common meeting ground, no club life. Most people are working so hard that they have lost the sense of going out. I sympathize. On my return from the studio I am often too tired to bestir myself. I regret this as so many vistas are waiting to be explored. The soaring towers of UCLA are almost across the road from me, and in this compound are enough art historians, scientists, philosophers and Nobel Prize winners to ornament the greatest seats of learning. A friend told me of how

* University of California, Los Angeles.

she found herself at a dinner of nuclear scientists who are involved with plans to land on the moon. Although they never talked of their secret life, yet somehow they gave the impression of already being on a different planet from the rest of us. Sometimes it is possible to prise Stravinsky, Henry Miller, Christopher Isherwood or Gerald Heard out of their lairs, but habit is strong and the isolationists hurry to get back to their work.

Friday

My contract is up. There were times when I doubted if I would ever reach the end of this stint. Even now, I feared last minute emergencies and changes of plan would keep me to new grind-stones. However, I was planning on a precipitous get-away. I woke early in order to finish the seemingly endless packing, to dismantle my hotel bed-sitter, to unpin the pictures off the bulletin boards, and to send back the small octagonal room into the anonymity in which I found it so long ago. Even though I would only dump my belongings into available boxes and cartons for the kind Eleanor Abbey to repack carefully at the studio, the mountain of stuff which has accumulated during the year has become a sort of Himalayan range.

I went to pay my bill and collect my diaries from the hotel safe, (seven notebooks have been filled since my arrival.) Back to the octagonal room for a valedictory glance round. For the last time I took to the freeway with its larva-like mountains rising forlornly each side of the eight parallel lanes of cement and tarmac.

(Extra care not to have an accident this morning.) The mile-stones passed: the signpost to Bakersfield, the fork to the Holly-wood and Ventura freeways: the hill going down to the San Fernando valley; today the customary blanket of pepper-coloured smog had been swept away by a gale, and in the bright sunlight Hollywood appeared as it used to in the pioneer days. 'Are you looking for a used spinet?' For the last time I was listening to Manning's Piano Parade. Then came the Seeley mattress news.

Here again the familiar white railings and sharp curve to the right where a forest of pampas grass has seeded itself. At this juncture the traffic always becomes dense, now it was almost at a standstill, and one could see red lights flashing in the distance which portended an accident. A truck of sand overturned, perhaps? Or lemons, or eggs? But no, the hold-up was due to 'Construction', and soon the congestion of traffic eased, Bullocks' offices with its vast parking grounds for personnel was passed. Van Nys Boulevard, Cold Water Canyon, Magnolia: only a few miles more now, and we veer off the freeway at Pass Avenue to Burbank. Thank God, safe arrival at the éclair-coloured bungalow!

A barrage of king-size Manilla envelopes was piled on my desk. Here were photographs from past, and almost forgotten, sittings. The pile was heightened with more packages arriving by 'special messenger'. Here were the long-awaited results of Bina Rothschild's and Gladys Cooper's sittings, here were the proofs of jolly Jack Warner himself. My room became a factory with messengers and bundles arriving and leaving every ten minutes. I worked like a steel automaton. Messengers were not available quick enough. George from the Still lab brought the colour transparencies of the paintings I'd done of the cast. Then Anne Laune telephoned to say goodbye and ask me one final question: 'How should we dress Doolittle's bride waiting at the "Church On Time"?' I made a sketch while Mort Lichter came to choose the photographs he would like to have for publicity. Before the morning's work was over four friends from Publicity called to take me out to a valedictory lunch. We talked of our hopes for the film and toasted each other in whiskey sours.

Back for the final round-up in my office. My baggage was bulging full and tight, extra packages had been done up to be sent air freight. Now I scribbled notes of goodbye – written messages often take less time than telephone calls. Then a farewell visit to the adorable people in the Wardrobe: Agnes' eyes melting; Louise, the salt of the earth and looking like Mother Earth; Carol, calm and cheerful with starry eyes. Anne Laune, with wrinkled forehead and eyes brimming over; Betty Huff, sweet and giggly and shivery; and Leah, a bulwark. In this Department I had spent the happiest moments since arriving. Here there was no one to say me nay, or interfere or put a damper on my activities. Here, only the most stimulating help.

To say goodbye to all these friends cost me much in emotional energy. But now I must muster the strength to go down on to Stage 7 and say goodbye to George Cukor and his Assistant Director, to thank Gene, and to take a fond farewell of Audrey.

They were shooting the scene where Eliza returns to Covent Garden Market after the row with Higgins. Eliza wore the Dolly Varden hat and the apricot coloured dress based on the costume in the Los Angeles museum. Her clothes superimposed sophistication onto a childlike waif, and somehow seemed to make her even more vulnerable. Eliza buys a bunch of violets from another flower girl, and looks at her with the expression on her face of 'there but for the grace of God ...' This is the sort of scene Audrey can do to perfection. She is at her best when portraying sweet sympathy and compassion. It was a somewhat archaic little pantomine that had been devised for her, but it was a nice note on which to leave. The shot was in the can. 'Save the lights.' Break for five minutes.

I crossed the cobblestones towards Audrey. She had put a Shetland shawl around her shoulders now, and looked forlorn. A few friends emerged from the crowd standing around. Geoff Allen and Virginia, Audrey's dresser, and red-haired Leonore, the hair-dresser, who had fought me so valiantly ...

Now adieu to Betsy, who looked very shy and twitched her nose when I kissed her farewell, and to Eleanor, bright-eyed with heart overflowing. The bags were all in the car, and now for the airport.

From my lair in Bel-Air I had often watched a red star crossing the evening sky. As my aeroplane now rose into the air, I knew I was part of the red star. From my window I looked down upon the Bel-Air district, Beverly Hills, then I watched as the vast carpet of twinkling Los Angeles lights left us far below.

Nearly a whole year has passed since I came out here to work on this project. But where have all those months gone? There has been little indication of the changing to spring to summer, and summer to fall: the seasons have passed imperceptibly in one long timeless stretch of intense routine activity. Perhaps the impersonal quality of these surroundings, artificially assembled on a desert has added to one's feelings of Nirvana. One's memory has few milestones to help on the way back to retrospect.

Of course the first impressions remain stronger than those in the haze of weeks that followed. It was particularly thrilling when, on arrival at the studio, one first started formulating vague plans which, by some sort of magic alchemy began to materialize. This period of gestation was, perhaps, the most satisfactory of all. The tempo mounted and results multiplied, and, by degrees, the date arrived when, at last, after six months' preparation, the camera started to grind on the pieces of our vast jigsaw puzzle.

I remember Hal Prince, on a visit from Broadway, warning me: 'Once the picture starts you're going to be bored. You've no idea how slow it is: you'll have done your job, and time'll hang heavy. One day you'll find the notice on your door has been taken down and the name of the next occupant installed. You'll be a forgotten man until the next time you're wanted for a new job.' It has not turned out like that for me. Until the last moment there have been ever more unexpected things to do. Work could be irksome, but details were new and would often come as a surprise.

No doubt about it, existence is comfortable in this cockaigne land. The climate slackens the nerves and induces a delightful *laisser aller*. An English actor said: 'You come out here, take a nap in the sun by the swimming pool, and wake up to find you are sixty-five!' But some of Hollywood's original *raisons d'être* have disappeared. The ubiquitous sun is seldom seen except as through a diffusing filter: Southern Californian news bulletins try to minimize the smog condition, but it is a serious problem. Gone, too, is the pervasive scent of orange-blossom – for the groves have been overbuilt. The flower markets that made such a welcome effect on the sidewalks have now disappeared indoors to the supermarkets.

If there are regrets they are far outweighed by the memory of so much that will remain pleasant long after the disappointments are forgotten. Yes, I am disappointed that none of the shots have been taken against the opal skies of London. There were some rough days on the set, but it is comforting to know, as Irwin Shaw has recently written in a devastatingly outspoken article, that the atmosphere in which a film is made is seldom reflected on the screen. How fortunate, too, I was in finding so many delightful people to make allowances for my being English. (Working in such close proximity, and under pressure, with so many types, I realize how far removed we are by the language barrier, by temperament and character!)

It was good fortune that brought me to work on a project with as great possibilities as these. It is not often a seventeen million dollar picture is made, and only once in a generation does a *My Fair Lady* occur. How often does a designer today have such an opportunity as the Ascot scene? Who is there better to dress than the impeccable Audrey Hepburn? It is warming to know that one has been part of an entertainment that is likely to give pleasure to so many.

Now, my own contribution made, the work has passed into the hands of tried experts who, for almost another year, will be working on cutting, scoring, polishing and refining the finished product, in an effort to place it on the highest peaks to which it is expected to attain.